# 40

## days with

# JESUS

**CWR**

**DAVE SMITH**
KINGSGATE COMMUNITY CHURCH

# ACKNOWLEDGEMENTS

I want to say a special thanks to a couple of people: to my daughter Annabel, who helped to write many of the Prayers and Points to ponder and to Canon J. John, who spent many hours rigorously critiquing and providing very valuable feedback. Thanks, also, to Pastor Simon Deeks for his suggestions, and to Dr Glenn Balfour, Principal, Mattersey Hall, who did a biblical proof-read.

Finally, a big thanks to the amazing church family at KingsGate for your love, prayers, support and encouragement. It's a joy to serve together.

Copyright © Dave Smith 2014
Published 2014 by CWR, Waverley Abbey House, Waverley Lane, Farnham, Surrey GU9 8EP, UK. CWR is a Registered Charity – Number 294387 and a Limited Company registered in England – Registration Number 1990308. Reprinted 2014 (twice), 2015 (twice).

Concept development, editing, design and production by CWR
Cover image: Istock/ Vetta Collection/PPAMPicture
Printed in the UK by Page Brothers
ISBN: 978-1-78259-138-2

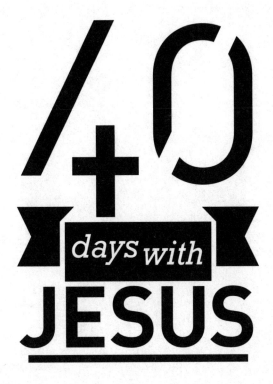

40
+
days with
JESUS

# CONTENTS

Acknowledgements     4

Foreword     7

Introduction     9

Week 1: A life-transforming encounter     13

Week 2: An eye-opening journey     33

Week 3: When Jesus comes in the midst     53

Week 4: Overcoming failure     77

Week 5: Made for a mission     99

Week 6: Final preparations     121

# FOREWORD

The four Gospel writers say something fascinating, but often overlooked, about the teaching, preaching and healing ministry of Jesus of Nazareth. They point out, with commendable honesty, that actually it was not really a success. True, the crowds gathered, listened, gawped at the miracles, but it seems that most of them soon went away. Yes, the crowds shouted praise of Jesus when He entered Jerusalem for the last time, but their enthusiasm seems to have been short lived. Matthew, Mark, Luke and John are united in saying that, by the time of His trial, Jesus stood alone and that at His dreadful death on the cross, His supporters were reduced to a handful of women and a single disciple. If you were reading through the Gospels without any other knowledge of Jesus you might assume, as you came to their closing pages, that what you had before you was simply yet another example of that depressingly familiar story: the good man who comes to a bad end.

Curiously though, historians tell us that within a few decades of the crucifixion there were people throughout the Roman Empire, some of them well educated, who considered Jesus to be alive – thought of Him as their constant day-to-day companion and prayed to Him as Lord and God. Within a couple of centuries a very large proportion of the Roman Empire had come to that conclusion.

It seems to me that these are two facts that cannot be denied. Yet taken together they pose an extraordinary problem. It is difficult to see how the life of Jesus of Nazareth could have ended in a more undignified, obscure and shameful manner. Those who watched the crucifixion must have felt that they were seeing the verdict of history or God, on Jesus: the cross showed that He was either a fraud or fool and certainly a failure and – just possibly – all three. Yet somehow, that judgment was reversed: disaster was turned to triumph, shame was turned to glory and the rejected, despised prophet was now declared to be the glorious King of the universe. Somehow, out of this most unpromising story, a radical, explosive new religion of hope and joy developed that swept everything before it. How on earth, we have to ask, did that happen?

The only satisfactory answer for this most astonishing of turnarounds lies in the resurrection of Christ; the 40 days discussed in this book. Those 40 days were *world-changing*. Without the resurrection it is doubtful whether anybody, other than a handful of experts in Jewish history of the period, would have even heard of Jesus of Nazareth. The resurrection was the explosion that propelled the new faith of Christ as God's Messiah out from Jerusalem into the world. It is the event that changed the world then and is still changing it today.

The historical significance of the resurrection is vital. It is an event that requires the greatest and most intense examination and this insightful book by my friend Dr David Smith covers the factual basis for believing in it. Yet the resurrection of Jesus is far more than that. It is not just a world-changing event but a *life-changing* event. Reject the resurrection and all you have in Jesus is yet another dead moral teacher in a world full of them. You can admire Him or try to follow some of His teachings and honour His memory. But that's all. Yet accept the resurrection and suddenly everything is changed. Jesus is no longer a dead figure, but somehow your contemporary. If you choose to trust Him and believe in Him, He goes along with you through all your days, whether they be filled with tears or triumphs. He is the one who befriends you, guides you, protect you and sometimes challenges you. He lives. If the resurrection is true, *everything changes* – life and death, hopes and fears, poverty and riches, aims and ambitions. All are changed by the existence of the living Christ.

I believe this is the only topic in history that can be described as both world-changing and life-changing. The 40 days between the first Easter Sunday and the ascension of Jesus into heaven deserve the most detailed attention we can give them. May this book help you to know the significance of those extraordinary days. They changed the world: may they change your life.

Canon J. John

# INTRODUCTION

## Why 40 days with Jesus?

I am so excited that you've decided to pick up this daily devotional. Over these next 40 days we will be focusing on the post-resurrection appearances of Jesus, from His appearing to Mary Magdalene on that first Resurrection Sunday morning through to His ascension to heaven nearly six weeks later.

These final days before Jesus ascended back to heaven were of such importance that all four Gospel writers included them in the conclusion of their account of Jesus' life (Matt 28, Mark 16,[1] Luke 24, John 20–21). In addition, Luke begins the sequel to his Gospel with a summary of the same period in Acts 1:1–11. Over the course of these 40 days, Jesus appeared to over 500 followers on at least 11 different occasions. Although it took the disciples some time to believe and embrace the full significance of Jesus' resurrection, ultimately, their personal encounters with the risen Christ completely changed their lives. This same message has the power to change our lives today, in the three following ways:

### 1.We can be **convinced of the reality** of the resurrection of Jesus

The primary purpose of the 40 days, then and now, was to provide vital evidence that Jesus really was and is alive, as Luke makes clear: 'After his suffering, he presented himself to them and gave them many *convincing proofs* that he was alive. He appeared to them over a period of forty days and spoke about the kingdom of God' (Acts 1:3, my emphasis). The certainty of the resurrection of Jesus became the foundation of the witness of those first disciples.[2]

So, today, as we spend time studying the main appearances recorded in the Gospels and Acts 1, we can become similarly convinced or re-convinced about the certainty of Jesus' resurrection, which is the very cornerstone of our faith.

## 2.We can be **transformed by encounters** with the risen Christ

The disciples encountered Christ physically during the 40 days; we can now do so spiritually. Since the ascension and the Day of Pentecost, Jesus is now present with His people in and through the power of the Holy Spirit, hence His wonderful promise at the very end of Matthew's Gospel: 'And surely I am with you always, to the very end of the age' (Matt. 28:20).

## 3.We can receive a **foretaste of our glorious future** in Christ

The post-resurrection appearances of Jesus provide the most comprehensive picture of what life will be like for us in our resurrected state. Jesus was and is the unique Son of God, but He is also the first-born of many sons and daughters who will be raised up in His likeness. The Jesus who appeared to His disciples was recognisably the same person, in the same physical body. Yet He was also clearly different, living in a body that was no longer restricted by the physical world.

If we look at the risen Jesus we see the foretaste of a life that is *not* a disembodied, purely spiritual existence, but rather a transformed physical life, with a glorified, resurrected body, in the new heavens and on the new earth!

So, as we study over the next 40 days, I have a three-fold prayer for you:

1. That your **faith** may be strengthened as you, like the first disciples, see convincing proofs that Jesus is alive and the true Lord of all.
2. That your **love** may be deepened as you, like the disciples on the Emmaus road, encounter the living and risen Christ through His Word, through His presence and through the breaking of bread.
3. That your **hope** may be increased as you get a foretaste of the future and of what life will be like when Christ returns.

# Final note

Although we will focus on the stories in the Gospels and the first chapter of Acts, it is worth noting that we also have compelling evidence from 1 Corinthians 15. This text is important because not only was it likely to have been written early (in AD 55), but Paul's evidence would have come from meetings with the other apostles that took place only a few years after the resurrection itself.[3] So, when he says 'for what I received I passed on to you of first importance' (1 Cor. 15:3), he is most likely referring to having talked to eyewitnesses around AD 35, only five years after the events themselves (AD 30). Paul's overview is therefore a very early source which confirms the later accounts found in the Gospels. The key elements of the narrative were: 'that Christ died for our sins according to the Scriptures, that he was buried, that he was raised on the third day according to the Scriptures, and that he appeared to Peter, and then to the Twelve. After that, he appeared to more than five hundred of the brothers at the same time, most of whom are still living, though some have fallen asleep. Then he appeared to James, then to all the apostles, and last of all he appeared to me also, as one abnormally born' (1 Cor. 15:3–8).

07

## A LIFE-TRANSFORMING
## ENCOUNTER

John 20:1–18

# A SURPRISING ENCOUNTER

## John 20:1

Have you ever had an encounter with another person that changed your life? I have, at least twice! The first was when I was at the baggage queue at Terminal 4 of Heathrow Airport. I was heading out to a kibbutz in Israel during my gap year, prior to going to university. Standing in the same baggage queue, I was immediately captivated by a beautiful girl called Karen. I quickly found out that she was going out to the same kibbutz. I fell in love almost immediately (it took her a little while longer!). Within a couple of months we were dating and three and a half years later we were married. That encounter definitely changed my life!

About six months later I had another surprising encounter that had an *even more* significant impact. I was now at university, and some people from the Christian Union invited me to a large church in the centre of Oxford called St Aldates. I remember little about the service apart from the final hymn. There, standing, singing along, I remember being suddenly aware of a loving 'presence' right there with me. For the first time in my life, I knew that the Jesus of my Sunday school days was real, and that by His unseen Spirit, He was calling me to come and follow Him. After several months of an internal battle, I finally yielded my life to God, and invited Christ to come into my life. Immediately my life was changed, and it continues to be changed to this day.

Throughout history, billions of people have been similarly changed by encounters with the risen Christ: during those 40 days through His physical appearances; since then through the power of His Holy Spirit.[4]

In Week 1 of this study we are going to focus on the first person to encounter the risen Jesus. Her name was Mary Magdalene.

This surprising and life-transforming event took place nearly 2,000 years ago. Jesus had just been crucified on what we know as Good Friday, when Mary, one of His devoted followers, went to visit His tomb early on Easter Sunday morning. So started the first post-resurrection encounter. We will explore this dramatic and poignant discovery throughout this week (John 20:1–18).

So who was this first witness of the empty tomb, and the first human being to see Jesus alive again? In recent times Mary Magdalene has become an increasingly popular and controversial character, being named in 2005 by *Newsweek* magazine as the 'It Girl' of our times. Yet this modern focus on Mary has only served to increase confusion as to her real identity. Many have wrongly assumed that she was the 'immoral' woman of Luke 7. Others, even more bizarrely and erroneously, believed that she was actually Jesus' wife. All that we can glean is that she was someone whose life had been one of oppression until she met Jesus who delivered her from 'seven demons' (Luke 8:2, Mark. 16:9). So radical was her conversion that she became a devoted and prominent follower of His, usually mentioned as the first in a list of female disciples. That was until her world was shattered by the trial, sufferings, death and burial of her Messiah, Jesus.

The fact that Mary was the first to witness the empty tomb, and then shortly afterwards the first to encounter the risen Christ, is highly surprising and significant. The other Gospel writers add that Mary was accompanied by other female disciples.[5] Either way, in a male-dominated culture, when the presence of female witnesses would not have been accepted in court, it is highly significant that the women were the first witnesses of the resurrection. If the early church and the Gospel writers had wanted to make up the story of the resurrection, they wouldn't have had the women there first![6] It is recorded this way, because that is what actually happened.

So why then was Mary first? The simple answer is because she was there first! She was clearly so devoted to Jesus that at the earliest opportunity after the Sabbath she got up to visit the tomb. Then, as we shall see, having witnessed the empty tomb, she was determined to find the body of Jesus, in contrast to the male disciples, who went home. Although Jesus eventually took the initiative and appeared to her, it seems as if this is in direct response to her loving, persistent seeking of Him.

So at the start of this study, it is important that we begin with the right attitude and, like Mary, diligently pursue the risen Jesus. Whether you are a seeker, a new believer, a struggling Christian or a fully devoted follower of Christ – know this: Jesus really is alive and is longing to meet with you.

---

## Points to ponder

- Are you convinced of the resurrection of Jesus? What difference would it make to your life and to the world at large if it were really true?
- What is your response to the idea that the risen Jesus wants to meet with you? In what ways would you like to meet with Jesus over the next 40 days?
- When have you encountered the presence of the living Jesus before? How did this impact you?

---

## Prayer

*Jesus, I realise that by asking about the implications of the resurrection for my life, I must be prepared to hear the answer. I cannot be the same and I don't want to be. I long to know You and meet with You. Take me on a journey over these next 40 days. Help me to be brave enough to respond to the things that You are whispering to me. Breathe Your life into any part of me that is currently lifeless or lacking in energy and spirit. Then move me forward by the power of Your Spirit in ways that only You can. I pray this in faith. Amen.*

# THE LIGHT OVERCOMES THE DARKNESS

---

## John 20:1

Most of us can identify with the phrase 'there's light at the end of the tunnel'. The 'darkness' of the tunnel helps convey situations that can seem particularly difficult or hopeless. Similarly we may encourage ourselves with the knowledge that the trial will eventually end and we will step into the 'light'. These trials can vary in nature and length, such as financial pressures, ill-health, and relational conflict. Our hope is that they will end quickly and that the 'light' will shine again on our world!

Hence when John starts his account of that first Easter Sunday morning by telling us that Mary Magdalene set out for the tomb of Jesus, 'Early on the first day of the week, *while it was still dark*' (John 20:1, my emphasis), he is not just telling us that it was very early in the morning. Rather, he is pointing out that something deeper is going on, at both an emotional and spiritual level. Just as in popular culture today, we have films like *Star Wars* with the forces of light triumphing over Darth Vader and 'the dark side' so, throughout his Gospel, John plays on the themes of light and darkness as representing the battle between good and evil. For example, in the early verses of chapter 1 he describes Jesus as the light who 'shines in the darkness, and the darkness has not overcome it' and as 'The true light that gives light to everyone' (John 1:5,9). Similarly, a couple of chapters later he declares: 'light has come into the world, but people loved darkness instead of light because their deeds were evil' (John 3:19). Even more tellingly for our present passage is the fact that when Judas went out to betray Jesus, John again pointedly lets us know that 'it was night' (John 13:30).

Hence, John's reference to darkness on that first Easter Sunday morning was intentional. For Mary, the shocking events of the torture, crucifixion and burial of Jesus would have plunged her into a dark tunnel from which there must have seemed no hope of a positive end. Her Lord and Saviour, her 'light' who had freed her from the powers of darkness, was now dead and defeated. It seemed as if the dark side – evil deeds, evil forces and evil people – had triumphed. It may also be that she was fearful that having been herself once gripped by the powers of darkness before she met Jesus, the 'darkness' would come back to imprison her now Jesus was no longer alive.

Yet, by the time Mary arrived at the tomb the scene was dramatically different from what she was expecting. Not only had the literal darkness of the early morning disappeared with the rising of the sun (Mark 16:2), but the heavy stone that had been placed to seal Jesus' dead body inside the dark tomb had been rolled away. Although neither Mary nor we as readers know the full implications of this, John is giving us the first indication that something momentous had happened: that the long tyranny of darkness was finally over, and that Jesus, the light and life of the world, had triumphed – a fact confirmed when Mary meets the risen Jesus.

This triumph of light over darkness is good news not just for Mary but for the whole of humanity. Each of us can now live in the 'light' of Jesus' earlier promise: 'I am the light of the world. Whoever follows me will never walk in darkness, but will have the light of life' (John 8:12). It may be that you are not yet a follower of Jesus and you are aware of things that are having an adverse effect on your life and your relationships. The good news is that because Jesus, the light of the world, really conquered darkness and death, you, like Mary, can be set free and can stay free. Maybe you are a Christian and you feel oppressed, or you know you have been set free from fear, shame or bondage in your life but you are concerned that these problems may return. If so, you can take heart! Because of the resurrection of Jesus, the darkness has gone, the light has come and a new day has dawned. Jesus really is alive, so you can really be free!

## Points to ponder

- Can you think of moments in your life when you were moved from darkness into light? What were the events leading up to this point? Take some time to thank God for His grace towards you during those times.
- Are there any areas of your life where you know that you are still living in darkness?
- Are there any places in your life where the light is on but is dim? How would your life change if you began to walk fully in the light in these areas?

## Prayer

*Jesus, I believe that You are the light of the world and I take hold of the promise that I never have to walk in the darkness when I am following You (John 8:12). Thank You for calling me out of the darkness and into Your wonderful light (1 Pet. 2:9). I reject any lie that may try to convince me that my breakthrough is not possible or will not be long-lasting. Freedom from sin and darkness is mine through Christ. I know that Your Word is a lamp for my feet and a light on my path (Psa. 119:105). Direct my steps and show me how to walk in the light. Lead me into freedom and keep me there! Amen.*

# LIFE OVERCOMES DEATH

## John 20:2–9

Death is humanity's greatest enemy. The last time I checked, the death rate was still 100 per cent! Throughout history men and women have unsuccessfully tried to overcome death. From the ancient Egyptian pharaohs who sought to escape death and go straight into the afterlife, through to our modern obsession with cosmetics and anti-ageing products, humanity has consistently tried and failed to overcome death and its effects. Whether we like it or not, we are all getting older and one day we will die! But that's not the end of the story.

The great news of Christianity is that because one man, Jesus of Nazareth, overcame death on that first Easter Sunday, those who believe in Him will one day share in His grave-overcoming life! Moreover, this resurrection hope is not just make-believe or wishful thinking; it is based on real factual evidence. In his Gospel, John dedicates two whole chapters (20–21) to giving us convincing proofs that Jesus had risen. From 20:1 we have already been made aware of the surprising fact of a woman as the first witness and of the fact that the huge stone guarding the tomb had been rolled away. Over the next few verses (20:2–9), John further builds his case by presenting us with three more key facts.

The first is that neither Mary nor the disciples were expecting the resurrection, and were therefore unlikely candidates to have pulled off a hoax, as some have simplistically suggested. Mary's immediate reaction to seeing the stone rolled away was not that Jesus had risen but that someone had taken his body: 'So she came running to Simon Peter and the other disciple, the one Jesus loved, and said, "They have taken the Lord out of the tomb, and we don't know where they have put him!"' (John 20:2). On hearing this news the two male disciples raced to the tomb, looked in and saw the grave clothes. Even though the 'other disciple' saw and believed,[7] John writes in parentheses: 'They still did not understand from Scripture that Jesus had to rise from the dead' (John 20:9). These reactions are understandable and entirely to be expected. Why? Because along with a key section of Jewish society, they would have believed in a final resurrection at the end of history, but they were not all prepared for the possibility that one person would rise in the middle of history. Clearly Jesus' previous teachings concerning His forthcoming resurrection had fallen on largely deaf ears!

The second fact presented here concerns the presence and positioning of the grave clothes within the tomb. As the 'other disciple' entered the tomb he 'bent over and looked in at the strips of linen lying there but did not go in. Then Simon Peter came along behind him and went straight into the tomb. He saw the strips of linen lying there' (John 20:5–6). This evidence is crucial. If the body had been stolen, the thieves would have taken the entire mummy because the clothes were the most valuable part. Yet here we have Jesus' body gone, with the grave clothes not even unwrapped, rather like a collapsed chrysalis. Unlike Lazarus earlier in the Gospel (John 11:44), who needed his grave clothes unwrapped, it seems as if Jesus had simply passed through them unaided.

The third fact concerns the head cloth or turban: 'the cloth that had been wrapped around Jesus' head ... was still lying in its place, separate from the linen' (John 20:7). It is not clear why John included this specific detail, other than that he is recording what the disciples saw first-hand. It does further emphasise that we are not talking about a grave robbery here, and we are left with the unmistakable picture that Jesus' body had gone, never to return.

This is further confirmed by the fact that, unlike many historical figures or religious leaders, Jesus' followers never venerated His tomb. Indeed, there is no evidence that after Easter Sunday morning, they ever went back there at all. Why? Because it was clear, then and now, that Jesus' body was no longer in the tomb!

## Points to ponder

- Consider the evidence given for the resurrection of Jesus in John 20:2–9. Which fact or facts do you find most convincing or compelling?
- Are you living in a way that reflects the reality of the resurrection?
- How do you feel about the fact that because Jesus has triumphed over death, you can have eternal life?

## Prayer

*Jesus, thank You that You have provided convincing proofs of Your resurrection. I rejoice that You didn't stay in the tomb but rose from the dead. I invite You to make Yourself known to me today. Grant me a spirit of wisdom and revelation that I might have a deep and lasting conviction of the historical reality of the resurrection. Amen.*

# JESUS IS PRESENT IN DESPAIR

## John 20:10–14

Despair is a cruel enemy that affects all of us at some time. Statistics show that in any given year, one in four Britons will face some form of mental distress, from acute anxiety through to depression. You may be facing the loss of a job; or a loss of purpose within your job. Perhaps you are mourning the loss of a relationship that was important. Maybe, like Mary, you have actually lost a loved one and it feels like your world has caved in. Or perhaps everything outwardly seems fine and yet you feel a real sense of inner emptiness.

The following paints a picture of Mary's despair: 'Then the disciples went back to where they were staying. Now Mary stood outside the tomb crying. As she wept, she bent over to look into the tomb, and saw two angels in white, seated where Jesus' body had been, one at the head and the other at the foot. They asked her, 'Woman, why are you crying?' 'They have taken my Lord away,' she said, 'and I don't know where they have put him.' At this, she turned round and saw Jesus standing there, but she did not realise that it was Jesus (John 20:10–14).'

The impression we get is that Mary was so blinded by her grief that she failed to see the signs that God had given her. Unlike the 'other disciple' for whom the sight of the empty tomb was enough to cause Him to believe in the resurrection (John 20:4–8), Mary was simply intent on finding the missing, dead body of Jesus.

It's the same for us too. Sometimes God gives us signs – clues of His presence – but because of our despair we, like Mary, fail to recognise Him. Yet God loves persistently, and in His grace He gave Mary two further signs.

The first sign was the presence of angels. All four Gospel writers tell of angels at the resurrection: only John has two angels stationed inside the tomb, where Jesus' head and feet would have been.[8] The presence of these heavenly 'messengers' should have indicated to Mary that somehow heaven had invaded the tomb, and that Jesus' disappearance from the tomb was the work of God, not people. Yet in her deep despair Mary failed to read the first clue.

She also initially failed to understand the second even more obvious sign; when Jesus *Himself* appeared to her: 'she did not realise that it was Jesus'. It's as if her grief and despair were such that even when Jesus Himself was right there with her, trying to get her attention, she failed to recognise him!

When we are in the middle of the most troublesome and distressing of circumstances, we so easily fail to realise that Jesus is standing there right with us by His Spirit. This should encourage us whenever we are facing difficulties of any kind. First, we need to realise that the Jesus we are speaking about is not aloof from, or put off by, our distress. Rather, He is a real man who understands our suffering since He too suffered (Heb. 2:14–18). Secondly, because He is now alive and present with us by His Holy Spirit we can experience His presence, comfort and help. Even if we struggle to sense His presence or hear His voice, we can be assured that He is with us.

If right now you are in the middle of a particularly troubling time and are filled with despair, can I encourage you to turn to Jesus? He is real and He is near, and He wants to help you, heal you and reveal Himself to you. There are numerous encouragements throughout the Bible that God is with us at all times, including the toughest. Let me conclude with one particular passage from Isaiah: 'Don't be afraid, I've redeemed you. I've called your name. You're mine. When you're in over your head, I'll be there with you. When you're in rough waters, you will not go down. When you're between a rock and a hard place, it won't be a dead end—Because I am God, your personal God, The Holy of Israel, your Savior' (Isa. 43:1–3, *The Message*).

The great news is that because Jesus is alive and His Spirit is here on the earth, we can know this God personally with us and in us forever!

## Points to ponder

- Are you in despair? Do you believe that God's love can overcome any pain or hopelessness you are facing? Is there someone you could ask to pray with you?
- Have you noticed any patterns in your life where similar circumstances consistently cause you to feel down or depressed? How can you increase your awareness of the presence of Jesus?
- Do you know anyone who is currently in despair? Take some time to pray for them.

## Prayer

*Lord, I want to reaffirm my commitment to You. I choose to put my trust in You today despite what I am facing or how I am feeling. You know every broken place in my life. You are intimately aware of my hurts and You keep a track of all of my sorrows. (Psa. 56:8). Jesus, because You became like me, fully human in every way (Heb. 2:17), I know that You identify with me. Open my eyes to recognise You in the midst of my brokenness. I believe that if I seek You with all my heart, I will find you (Jer. 29:13). Yet, I thank You that You seek after me too. With Your tender love, come and lead me from despair into hope, from anxiety into peace and from brokenness into wholeness. Amen.*

Day

# 05 HEARING HIS VOICE

## John 20:15–16

Today, we come to one of the most moving and significant events in history: the moment when Jesus first showed Himself alive to another human being. It is also important for another reason. It highlights that the *way* Jesus chose to reveal Himself to Mary is the way He reveals Himself to us today: by speaking to us!

We pick up the story with Mary in the garden outside the 'empty' tomb, so distressed that she fails to recognise Jesus when He does appear. That is until Jesus graciously and tenderly engages her in conversation: 'He asked her, "Woman, why are you crying? Who is it you are looking for?" Thinking he was the gardener, she said, "Sir, if you have carried him away, tell me where you have put him, and I will get him." Jesus said to her, "Mary." She turned towards him and cried out in Aramaic, "Rabboni!" (which means 'Teacher')' (John 20:15–16).

It is first worth pausing to highlight how necessary the post-resurrection appearances were to convince Mary and the other disciples. It is one thing not to be in the tomb but another to actually show yourself alive!

Secondly, it is important to grasp how we are to understand this incident. Mary is not seeing just a vision, a ghost or something that she has conjured up in her agitated imagination. Rather this is someone who is a real person, whom she at first mistakes for the gardener, who engages her in real conversation, who knows her name, and who has a physical body that can be touched.

Thirdly, and of huge importance for us today, is the way that Jesus revealed Himself: 'Mary'. That was all it took for her eyes to be opened. At the sound of her name, at the recognition of His person and the realisation that He was alive, Mary's world was changed forever. Why does she recognise Him when He speaks, rather than when she sees Him? Part of the answer lies in John's earlier portrayal of Jesus as the good shepherd: 'He calls his own sheep by name and leads them out. When he has brought out all his own, he goes on ahead of them, and his sheep follow him because they know his voice' (John 10:3–4). Jesus, the good shepherd, who knows His sheep by name, called Mary's name, leading her out from darkness into light and from despair into hope. Just as the sheep recognise the voice of the shepherd, so Mary recognises Jesus when He speaks to her and calls her by name.

It is highly significant that the first person to 'see' Jesus recognised Him first through His voice rather than through His physical appearance. There are, of course, instances during the 40 days when Jesus is recognised first by His physical appearance. There have also been occasions throughout history – such as with Saul on the road to Damascus and in certain countries today where there is open hostility to the gospel – where Jesus shows Himself as the risen living Lord. Yet, Jesus' appearance to Mary sets a pattern for life beyond the ascension. This new way of recognising and believing reaches a climax in the encounter between Jesus and Thomas in John 20:29: 'blessed are those who have not seen and yet have believed.' (More of this in Week 3.)

Whether you know Him or not, whether you know Him well or a little, know this: Jesus is alive, He knows you by name and wants to speak to you through His Word and by His Spirit, calling you into a new and deeper experience of, and relationship with, Himself.

## Points to ponder

- What an incredible thought that God Almighty, the King of the heavens, knows you and me by name! Do you need to hear Jesus call your name?
- How aware are you that Jesus is a real person, with thoughts, feelings, a personality and a voice? What difference does this make to the way you can relate to Him?
- How will you live differently today knowing that Jesus is present with you right now by the Holy Spirit? Just as Jesus spoke to Mary in her despair, so He can and will speak to you, too. The great news is that your 'lows' can be made 'highs' by God!

## Prayer

*Jesus, I thank You for caring enough about me to call my name. I thank You that You are with me today through the Holy Spirit. Holy Spirit, I welcome You into my life and ask that You would make real to me the presence of Jesus in a fresh way. I am honoured that You would choose to make Your home in my heart. Show me how I can host You and Your presence today and every day. Help me to be sensitive to Your voice. Amen.*

# RELATIONSHIP REDEFINED

—

## John 20:17–18

Yesterday we saw how the appearance of the risen Jesus to Mary set the pattern for a new way of encountering Him: through hearing His voice. Today, we will look at another crucial aspect of their redefined relationship: a change that has huge implications for us, too.

Clearly thrilled to see Jesus, Mary clings on to Him, an action that invokes this important response from Jesus: 'Do not hold on to me, for I have not yet ascended to the Father. Go instead to my brothers and tell them, "I am ascending to my Father and your Father, to my God and your God"' (John 20:17).

It is important to note that Jesus is not rebuking her for touching Him (as many medieval and Renaissance painters of this scene pictured it); rather He was telling her to let go because she was clinging on to Him. The reason for this is found in the phrase: 'for I have not yet ascended to the Father.' Whatever else this may have meant, what seems clear is that Jesus is saying that from now on Mary was not to relate to Jesus in the same way that she had always done – by seeing, touching and speaking to Him in His earthly body. Why? Because Jesus was going to heaven to be with the Father. However, rather than see this as a loss, He introduces news of a glorious transformation in the message that she is entrusted to bring to the disciples: 'I am ascending to my Father and your Father, to my God and your God.' The point seems clear. At the heart of the gospel is this staggering message. Although Jesus was and is the unique Son of God, now through His death and resurrection, He has become our elder brother (Heb. 2:11) and God is now our Father.

We need to pause for a moment and let this sink in. Here, Jesus is introducing the glory of our spiritual adoption. In *Knowing God*, author J.I. Packer poses the question: 'What is a Christian?' and answers 'A Christian is one who has God as Father.'[9] When you became a Christian, you did not join a religion, a denomination or a movement. You joined a family that will last forever.

There is no higher privilege.

Yet it doesn't end here. The first thing that Mary is to do in response to this glorious news is to go and tell the other disciples ('my brothers'). This highlights an important point. Our spiritual adoption is not something that we selfishly hold on to. Rather, we ought to extend this relationship to others. Immediately Mary is faithful to this gospel call: 'Mary Magdalene went to the disciples with the news: "I have seen the Lord!" And she told them that he had said these things to her' (John 20:18).

----

## Points to ponder

- What is your response to the idea that God is your Father?
- When you pray or worship God, how do you see yourself approaching Him: do you see yourself as an undeserving sinner coming to a reluctant God or, as God sees you, as a much loved child, coming to a wonderful Father who loves you very much?

----

## Prayer

*Jesus, thank You for welcoming me into Your family. I thank You for bridging a way for me to come to the Father. I thank You that all who receive You and believe in Your name have the right to become children of God (John 1:12) and co-heirs with You (Rom. 8:17). Father, Your Word says that You are perfect (Matt. 5:48). You are far better than any earthly father. You do not disappoint or falter. You will never leave me or forsake me (Deut. 31:6). You long to lavish Your love on me (1 John 3:1). As Your child, I receive Your love afresh today. Thank You for Your faithfulness to me. Help me to be faithful in telling others the good news. Amen.*

# SEEKING AND FINDING

## John 20:1–18

Looking back over the previous week, what can we learn from the example of Mary and her encounter with Jesus?

Firstly, we can be inspired by Mary's pursuit of Jesus. Mary was the first to go to the tomb. She was also the last to leave. It is surely no accident that the one who sought after Jesus the most was the first to see Him risen.

Throughout Scripture, we are encouraged to persistently and fervently seek God (see Prov. 8:17). In the Gospels, Jesus Himself exhorts us: 'seek and you will find' (Luke 11:9). All of this highlights the importance of diligently seeking God. Since He is the greatest person in the universe, knowing Him, encountering Him, and communing with Him is the highest privilege and pleasure available. Hence, it is worth our greatest efforts. As we continue through the rest of these 40 days, can I encourage you to seek after the risen Christ in these practical ways:

- **Find the time** – although we can meet with God at any time, there is something about setting aside particular time to meet with Him. Choose the time of the day when you are at your best and be consistent in this.
- **Find the place** – again, the Lord can and will meet us anywhere, but there is something about finding a place or places where you will be undisturbed and where you can meet with Him in a more intimate way.
- **Find the way** – there are many ways to meet with the Lord and develop your relationship with Him. Yet, the two primary ways are to spend time listening to Him by daily, diligent and devotional reading and reflecting on His Word; and by speaking to Him in worship and in prayer.

If you need help in learning how to meet with Christ through daily Bible reading, then I would recommend a book by Wayne Cordeiro, called *The Divine Mentor*. If you're not sure how to get started in prayer, then the best place to start is the Lord's prayer. If you would like to listen to some teaching to help you pray through the Lord's prayer, then you can find the series 'How to pray' on the KingsGate website: www.kingsgateuk.com Remember the promise: if we seek Him diligently, we will, like Mary, find Him!

Secondly, we can be encouraged by Jesus' seeking after Mary! Just as He gave Mary unmistakable proofs of His presence, so He wants to reveal Himself to us today. There were the initial signposts: the rolled away stone, the missing body from the tomb, the collapsed grave clothes, the separate head cloth and the angels. Then there was the actual encounter when He took the initiative to appear to her, speak to her and reveal Himself to her. It is the same with us. While it may seem as if we are seeking Him, when we step back and ponder, we can see that all along He was first seeking us – leaving us signposts of His presence and then revealing Himself to us by calling us by name and speaking to us personally and intimately.

----

## Points to ponder

- How can you more diligently seek after Jesus on a daily basis?
- Encourage yourself with the fact that He is already taking the initiative to seek after you!

----

## Prayer

*Lord Jesus, I thank You that You are pursuing me. I respond to Your initiative. Help me to find the time, the place and the way to meet with You most effectively. Reveal Yourself and increase Your presence in my life, I pray. Amen!*

# 02

## AN EYE-OPENING JOURNEY

Luke 24:13–35

# Day
# 08

# VISION CORRECTION SURGERY

## Luke 24:13–16

For the first 19 years of my life, I was spiritually blind. I grew up in a vicarage, spent six years living in a Christian community, attended Sunday school, went to Christian youth groups and sat through countless church services. But it was all a bit of a blur! While not intellectually disagreeing with what I was hearing, it was as if I had a spiritual veil over my eyes, so that the reality and significance of who Christ was and why He came, didn't really impact me.

After a brief period of searching at the age of 11–12, I gave up, stopped going to church and embarked on a full-scale teenage rebellion. That was until my first year of university, when I had what I would describe as vision correction surgery: my eyes were opened, and for the first time I could actually 'see' my true need of Christ and appreciate what He had really done for me.

Throughout history God has specialised in opening the eyes of people. A particularly dramatic 'eye-opening' journey took place on the first Easter Sunday afternoon. Two of Jesus' disciples were 'going to a village called Emmaus, about seven miles from Jerusalem' (Luke 24:13). We know that one of these was called Cleopas (v18), and the other is unnamed. Since they are going 'home' (vv28–29), it is possible that the other one is Cleopas' wife, Mary, mentioned in all four Gospels as being present at the crucifixion. The fact that they are clearly not among 'the Twelve' apostles highlights the authenticity of the incident. If it was a made up account, the writer would surely have described it as happening to somebody more well-known.

Luke records how: 'As they talked and discussed ... with each other, Jesus himself came up and walked along with them; but they were kept from recognising him' (Luke 24:14–16). There are different possible reasons why the disciples may have failed to recognise Jesus. It may partly be, as with Mary Magdalene, that it was because the risen Jesus, although the same person, looked somehow different. Yet the phrase 'kept from' indicates some power at work. One commentator has suggested that this was Satan keeping them spiritually blind; others that God Himself was doing so. But as we shall see, it was also the attitude of the disciples themselves that caused a partial blindness or blurring of their spiritual vision – attitudes that we will unpack over the next couple of days.

What is most encouraging, however, is that Christ took the initiative to come to these disciples. Although they may not have been able to recognise Him at first, He nevertheless joined them on their journey and 'walked along with them'. As I look back on my own journey, I now realise that there were times in my childhood and early teens when Christ was particularly present, walking along with me by His Spirit, but I failed to recognise Him. I am so glad that in His love He persisted until my eyes were finally opened!

Throughout history, Christ has specialised in coming to people, and in His persistent grace, engaging them until they see Him for who He is. One of the most famous conversions in history was that of John Newton (1725–1807), the former slave trader. In his early 20s he was on his way back from America when his ship encountered a storm and he almost drowned. Newton called on God, the ship drifted to safety, and he started a journey of reading the Bible and other evangelical literature, until he was finally converted. He went on to serve Christ, eventually becoming a leading campaigner for the abolition of the slave trade and a friend of William Wilberforce. In his famous hymn *Amazing Grace*, he includes these words: 'I once was lost but now I'm found, was blind but now I see!'

The great news is that throughout history, billions of people have also had an 'eye-opening' journey with Jesus: not physically as did these two on the Emmaus road, but rather, spiritually, such as in the case of John Newton. The even better news is that you and I can also have either a first-time or fresh encounter with Jesus, by His Holy Spirit. That encounter could happen today!

## Points to ponder

- Have you begun an eye-opening journey with Jesus?
- How clear is your vision of the risen Jesus?
- Is your vision blurred in any way? Sometimes we fail to see something because of our own 'eye defect', sometimes we fail to see because we have put something in front of our eyes. Is there something that you have let obscure your vision?

## Prayer

*Jesus, I thank You that You want to reveal Yourself to me, so that I can 'see' who You really are and what You have done for me. Please remove anything from me that is obscuring my vision of You. I ask You to give me Your Spirit of wisdom and revelation so that I can know You. Amen.*

# VISION BLURRED BY DISAPPOINTMENT

---

## Luke 24:17–21

Proverbs 13:12 says that 'Hope deferred makes the heart sick'. Without hope we can quickly fall into a downward spiral of apathy, depression and feeling purposeless, which can prevent us from seeing the Lord and His purpose for our lives.

In our story of the two disciples on the Emmaus Road, it seems as if, like Mary Magdalene earlier that day, their acute sense of disappointment and despair had prevented them from recognising Jesus. In a scene of irony, Jesus comes alongside them and initiates a conversation, where they express their disappointment concerning the 'failure' of Jesus and His mission, with Him alive and right there with them: 'He asked them, "What are you discussing together as you walk along?" They stood still, their faces downcast. One of them, named Cleopas, asked him, "Are you the only one visiting Jerusalem who does not know the things that have happened there in these days? … Jesus of Nazareth … was a prophet, powerful in word and deed before God and all the people. The chief priests and our rulers handed him over to be sentenced to death, and they crucified him; but we had hoped that he was the one who was going to redeem Israel"' (Luke 24:17–21).

The phrase 'we had hoped' highlights their acute feelings of disappointment. The death of Jesus on the cross seemed to symbolise the death of their hopes that He would redeem Israel from her political and military enemies.The fact that He had not only died, but had died an utterly shameful death on a cross, made it seem highly unlikely that He was a prophet of God, let alone the Messiah. The irony, of course, is that it was *because* of the cross and the fact that Jesus paid the *ransom price* with His own blood, that not just Israel, but the whole world could be freed from the spiritual slavery to sin, self and Satan.[10] Their misplaced sense of disappointment blinded them to the reality of the fact that He who is the resurrection and the life was walking alongside them.

Part of the problem was that the disciples had decided that God was going to work one way, with Jesus the Messiah King ruling from Jerusalem. Their fixation with this made them overlook the possibility that actually God was intending to work in another, far better way. Equally, we can fall into the trap of being so absolutely certain that God is going to do one thing that we completely overlook the possibility of a different and better solution. While not everything in life works out, the message of the cross is that what can sometimes look like huge disappointment and total defeat may actually be the gateway to great hope and victory.

I remember the huge sense of disappointment that we had to face when we lost planning permission for a church building in Peterborough. Quickly, I sensed the Lord letting me know that He was still very much with us and was in charge, and that I was to shrug off disappointment and encourage the congregation to do likewise. When a year or so later we had secured planning on a site that was in a far better location, and double the size, I realised that God had something better all along.

Regardless of our immediate circumstances and how things will work out, we must not stay in a place of disappointment. If we do, we will lose our vision and perspective of who Christ is and what He has accomplished. None of us is immune from disappointment, which is part of living in a fallen world. Life is full of setbacks, yet God can and does use these to teach us things that prepare us for future glory. In the words of Martin Luther King, Jr: 'We must accept finite disappointment ... but we must never lose infinite hope.'

If right now, you are living with disappointment, know this: Jesus is present. So, don't lose hope.

## Points to ponder

- What are your 'I had hoped for' prayers or dreams? Don't give up on these. Commit these to the Lord: ask for His grace to persevere and for His plan to unfold in the right time.
- Don't allow your sense of disappointment to prevent you from expecting God to work in your life. Is it possible that your desire to see God acting in a particular way has blinded you to the possibility that God might be acting in some other way?
- Are you disappointed with anyone? Are you disappointed with yourself? Acknowledge this and then release it to the Lord. Ask for His forgiveness for holding on to these things and ask that His Holy Spirit will fill you with grace to move forward.

## Prayer

*Jesus, I thank You that hopelessness and disappointment are not my inheritance. I will not allow my hope to be stolen because I know that You cause all things to work together for my good (Rom. 8:28). I release all sense of disappointment to You now. Amen.*

# VISION BLURRED BY DOUBT

---

## Luke 24:22–24

As we continue on our 'eye-opening journey' with Jesus on the Emmaus Road, we will look today at the problem of doubt and unbelief. If disappointment can cause the blurring of our spiritual vision, doubt can cause partial or near total spiritual blindness. Later, in Week 3, we will look in more detail at the dangers of unbelief and the importance of faith, with the story of Thomas. For now, it is worth being alert to how doubt can prevent us from 'seeing' Jesus, wherever we are in our spiritual journey.

It seems as if the main reason why the disciples failed to recognise Jesus on the Emmaus Road, even though He was standing right there with them, was because of their unbelief. In spite of reports of an empty tomb and angels declaring that Jesus was really alive, they still didn't believe (Luke 24:22–24). It is quite clear that according to Jesus this doubt and unbelief was at the root of their spiritual problem and He rebuked them for it: 'How foolish you are, and how slow to believe all that the prophets have spoken! Did not the Messiah have to suffer these things and then enter his glory?' (Luke 24:25–26).

This is a hugely important section in understanding how Jesus reveals Himself to humanity. Notice what He doesn't do. He doesn't rebuke the disciples for not believing the reports concerning the empty tomb. He doesn't at this point say: 'Don't be stupid, it's me, Jesus!' He doesn't draw their attention to His physical presence, rather He directs them to what the Old Testament Scriptures say about Himself, His suffering and entering into glory.[11]

The main reason why the disciples failed to recognise the risen Jesus on the Emmaus Road was because they were intellectually and spiritually unprepared for the possibility that the one they had seen crucified could actually have been resurrected. Like the disciples in John 20:9, they had failed to understand 'from Scripture' that Jesus had to die and rise from the dead.

This is significant, not just for the disciples then, but for us today. In one sense, it means that we are on a level playing field. While we don't have the opportunity to physically 'see' Jesus alive, we have not only the Old Testament Scriptures, but also now the New Testament eyewitness accounts of the resurrection. As we shall see tomorrow, Jesus directs His disciples then and now to the Scriptures as the first point of reference in proving that He was and is alive. In the same way, today, we need the help of the Holy Spirit to apply God's Word to our lives.

Wherever you are on your spiritual journey, it is important to realise that doubt and unbelief concerning what the Bible says about Jesus is the primary hindrance to 'seeing' Him for who He really is. The good news is that no matter how blurred your spiritual vision, or how spiritually blind you are, there is a cure ...

---

## Points to ponder

- How would you define doubt?
- In what ways can unbelief in the resurrection hinder faith in Christ?
- Are there any particular areas of your life where you find it more difficult to believe the promises of God, such as for healing, provision, answers to prayer etc? How might you grow in faith in these areas?

---

## Prayer

*Lord, I ask You to forgive me for where I have doubted and been slow to believe. Holy Spirit, will You come and shine Your light into the darkness of my mind and reveal Christ to me? Amen.*

# Day 11

# VISION CORRECTED BY A REVELATION OF THE SCRIPTURES

## Luke 24:25–27,32

Over the past three days we have been looking at how, like the disciples on the Emmaus Road, our vision of Jesus can be blurred by, among other things, disappointment and doubt. The great news, however, is that the story has a happy ending. Like them, our vision can be corrected and our spiritual eyes can be opened.

The first way that our vision is corrected is through a revelation of Christ in the Scriptures. As we saw yesterday, Jesus' primary rebuke focused on the disciples' failure to believe 'all that the prophets have spoken'. He then went on to show them how the Old Testament Scriptures pointed to Himself: 'And beginning with Moses, and all the Prophets, he explained to them what was said in *all* the Scriptures *concerning himself*' (Luke 24:27, my emphases).

The only Bible that the disciples and Jesus had would have been the Old Testament. Today, we have the added and wonderful benefit of having the New Testament as well – of which Jesus is, of course, the main character. In the words of the former Bishop of Rochester, Dr Christopher Chavasse: 'The Bible is the portrait of our Lord Jesus Christ. The Gospels are the figure itself in the portrait. The Old Testament is the background leading up to the divine figure, pointing towards it and absolutely necessary to the composition as a whole. The Epistles serve as the dress ... explaining and describing it. Then, while by our Bible reading we study the portrait as a great whole, the miracle happens, the figure comes to life and stepping down from the canvas of the written word, the everlasting Christ of the Emmaus story becomes himself our Bible teacher, to interpret to us in all the Scriptures the things concerning himself.'[12]

The key point here is that Christ wants to reveal Himself to us through the Scriptures. If this is true, we can expect that this will apply not just to the start of our spiritual journey, but to our ongoing journey with Him. I know that for me, and for countless Christians throughout the ages, daily Bible reading, reflecting on what has been read, followed up by prayerful application, has been a primary source of revelation and transformation, as Jesus increasingly makes Himself known through the ever-present Holy Spirit.

As a KingsGate church family, we recently took part in a spiritual health survey called 'Reveal'. The striking results from this survey of hundreds of churches worldwide, and tens of thousands of believers, is that the number one catalyst for spiritual growth and health was the practice of regularly reading and reflecting on Scripture. Just as Jesus first revealed Himself to these disciples on the Emmaus Road, so He wants to reveal himself to you and me as we daily and diligently read and reflect upon the Scriptures. As we do, we can be assured that the risen Christ will Himself come to us, and by the Holy Spirit will Himself become our Bible teacher.

Clearly this encounter with Christ through the Scriptures had a profound effect on these two disciples. After their eyes had been finally opened to see Christ as He broke bread with them, their immediate reflection was of His Bible teaching: 'Were not our hearts burning within us while he talked with us on the road and opened the Scriptures to us?' (Luke 24:32).

## Points to ponder

- Do you read the Scriptures daily? If so, how well are you connecting with the Lord during these times? If you are not reading the Bible each day, what changes can you make to your lifestyle to allow space to feast on His Word?*
- Maybe you are reading the Bible regularly, but it has become dry and routine. Why not take time to invite the Holy Spirit to be your Helper and to bring revelation, life and application as you read and reflect?
- How are you making sure you apply the Bible to your life? What adjustments have you made to your life as a result of reading the Bible recently?

## Prayer

*Thank You Father for the power of the written word to change my life. Holy Spirit, I ask You to increase my passion for reading and applying the Word to my life so that it becomes one of the chief delights of my day. As I read Your Word day by day, open the eyes of my heart that I might meet with You and come to know You more and more. It's You I want to meet, Lord Jesus. Amen.*

*Visit www.cwr.org.uk to find a range of daily Bible-reading notes.

# VISION CORRECTED BY WELCOMING HIS PRESENCE

## Luke 24:28–29

Here's the shocking truth. In spite of Jesus being on the journey with the two disciples on the Emmaus Road and personally taking time to reveal the Scriptures concerning Himself, they still could have missed Him! The key point to notice about the following incident is that Jesus was about to continue on with His journey: 'As they approached the village to which they were going, Jesus continued as if he were going farther. But they urged him strongly, 'Stay with us, for it is nearly evening; the day is almost over.' So he went in to stay with them' (Luke 24:28–29). It wasn't until they responded to His presence by showing Him hospitality and urging Him to come in and eat with them, that He actually revealed Himself to them.

I am reminded of a similar passage in the book of Revelation. Jesus is speaking: 'Here I am! I stand at the door and knock. If anyone hears my voice and opens the door, I will come in and eat with that person, and they with me' (Rev. 3:20). Jesus is knocking but He will only come in when invited! Moreover, He doesn't just want to come into the hallway; He wants to come into every room of our lives.

I read recently of how Jesus came knocking on the door of one of Britain's most successful entrepreneurs, Duncan Bannatyne.

'For me the tears came at about ten o'clock that night ... my face was wet, my nose began to run and I was a mess ... After many minutes I began to get the feeling that I wasn't alone. It was there that God said hello. I felt that I had been consumed by this presence, that something had completely shrouded and taken hold of me. It was unmistakable: I knew who had come and I also knew why. It wasn't a spiritual thing, it was a Christian thing, and I felt I was being told, "You've arrived, join the faith, be a Christian, this is it." It was profound, and I stood there, stunned, considering the offer and thinking about what it would mean. I knew I wanted to keep on making money, and I also knew I wanted to carry on doing all the things I wasn't proud of – I knew I was never going to be this totally Christian guy going to church on Sundays. So I said, "No, I'm not ready." And God said okay and disappeared.'[13]

How many people, like Duncan Bannatyne, have had similar opportunities, but have turned Christ down? The truth is that Christ comes knocking on each of our doors. Have you opened it yet? If not, then I want to invite you to pray in a moment and ask Him in. If you have opened the door, know that this is not just a one-off event. The Christian life really is a journey of increasing revelation and an ongoing, deepening awareness of Him. We have to actively welcome the presence of His Spirit. Jesus is there all the time, but when we pray and actively welcome Him, we become newly aware of His presence.

## Points to ponder

- Are there any 'rooms' of your life where you are struggling to open the door to Jesus? Why not make a choice this day to consciously open that door to Jesus?
- How conscious are you of the presence of the Spirit with you, moment by moment, during your day? What could you do to increase that sense of His presence?
- When you have your usual prayer times this week, be alert to those times when Jesus, by His Spirit, is inviting you to linger in His presence for a longer time.

## Prayer

*Lord Jesus, I thank You that You are lovingly knocking on the door of my life. Today, I make a choice to open the door and welcome You in to every part of me. Come and fill me and change me today, by the power of Your Holy Spirit. Amen.*

# VISION CORRECTED THROUGH THE BREAKING OF BREAD

## Luke 24:30–31,33–35

Today, we come to the climax of our 'eye-opening journey' by looking at the very moment when the eyes of the two disciples were fully and finally opened: 'When he was at the table with them, he took bread, gave thanks, broke it and began to give it to them. Then their eyes were opened and they recognised him' (Luke 24:30–31).

I love the contrast this meal has with the first 'meal' and 'eye-opening' in the Bible. In disobedience of God's command, Eve gave Adam some of the forbidden fruit, they both ate, their eyes were opened and they recognised their nakedness (Gen. 3:6–7). This first 'eye-opening' event had tragic consequences, bringing guilt, shame, disorder and death.

But here, on the first Easter Day, on the first day of the week, symbolising the start of the new creation, the perfect human, the resurrected Jesus, took bread, gave thanks, broke it and gave it to His disciples to eat.[14] No blinding flash of illumination or rebuke, but the gentlest of reminders over a meal. Now their eyes were opened *not to their shame*, but to the glory of the risen Jesus. This is great news then and now: the long curse has been reversed, the price for sin has been paid for – death itself has been defeated. Jesus really is alive, so we can really live!

The significance for today is that Jesus is revealed in the context of a fellowship meal. Although Jesus did appear to individuals (for example, Mary Magdalene and Peter), most often, as we shall see, He appeared to His disciples while they were gathered together in community. Presumably there was something about the way Jesus took bread, gave thanks, broke it and gave it to them, that reminded the disciples of previous communal meals or, indeed, of the feeding of the 5,000 (Luke 9:15–16). The fact that He first gave thanks for the bread is a salutary reminder that – especially as so many today go hungry – we must not take food for granted and not neglect the simple practice of saying 'grace' before meals. More broadly, this incident should increase our expectancy for Jesus to be present as we eat together in our homes, in His name.

Although today's passage depicts a fellowship meal (and not communion, as some have suggested), there are echoes of the Lord's Supper. The language here in Luke 24 – 'he took bread, gave thanks, broke it and began to give it to them' – is strikingly similar to His sharing of the Passover a few days earlier when he 'took bread, gave thanks and broke it, and gave it to them, saying, "This is my body given for you; do this in remembrance of me"' (Luke 22:19). There is of course no mention of Jesus' body being given, and no reference to wine in the Emmaus story, but the links were sufficient that Luke would have been encouraging the early Christians to expect Christ to reveal Himself as they took communion in the context of their fellowship meals together.

For us today, as we gather together in community, and as we celebrate our unity in Christ by breaking bread together, we can expect Christ to reveal Himself to us as He did to those two disciples on the Emmaus Road. As we ponder on His sacrifice we can expect that our vision will be corrected and our eyes will be opened to who He is and what He has done for us through His death – in truly redeeming us and freeing us from spiritual sin and slavery.

## Points to ponder

- It is good to be reminded that Jesus revealed Himself at a fellowship meal. Is eating together with other Christians something that is part of your lifestyle? Do you thank God for your food, and expect Christ to be present amongst you?
- If you are in a church that has small groups, and you are not part of such a group, can I encourage you to join one. Raise your expectation of meeting with Jesus as you gather and break bread together.
- Is there anyone with whom you know you are out of fellowship in any way? Do all you can, as it rests with you, to seek reconciliation with them.

## Prayer

*Lord I thank You for Your tenderness and gentleness towards us and that You revealed Yourself to the disciples over a meal. Forgive us when we have neglected the simple practice of eating together in Your name, and thanking You for the food we have. As we begin to eat together, and break bread, we ask You to reveal Yourself to us in new ways. Amen!*

# GO AND SHARE THE GOOD NEWS

## Luke 24:33–35

There's something about good news that's hard to keep to yourself.

When our second daughter got engaged, it was a very clear reminder of just how quickly and extensively good news travels! Within hours, not just the news that they had got engaged, but also pictures of the ring, and details of the location and nature of the proposal were being posted online and enthusiastically shared from person to person. Sharing good news with others really is a joyful and natural thing to do.

So, it is no surprise to see the excited and overjoyed disciples immediately sharing the greatest news of all concerning the resurrection of Jesus. Mary Magdalene's first response to seeing the empty tomb and the risen Jesus was to go and tell the other disciples. Similarly, the first response of the two Emmaus disciples was to return immediately to Jerusalem to tell the others. There is nothing forced or reluctant about this sharing. Why? Because good news is easy to talk about!

I remember when I first became a Christian. I was so thrilled with what God had done for me that I immediately shared it with family and friends – some of whom later became Christians, too. Then I began to share it with strangers – on the streets, on trains, on buses, in fact wherever there were people I felt compelled to share the good news, often whether they wanted to hear it or not! Although I had much to learn about sensitivity and wisdom, at the time it felt like it was the most natural and obvious thing to do. There have been seasons when I have become dulled in my passion for evangelism. Yet, still thirty years later, I regularly seek opportunities to tell others. Why? Because I want them to know Him, too!

I know that for many Christians the prospect of 'witnessing' can appear scary. Others hide behind personality differences, suggesting that verbal proclamation of the gospel is only for bold people. But just as the good news of my daughter's engagement was shared quickly and spontaneously by all types of people, so too, we need to rediscover the wonder of the gospel message and learn how to naturally (supernaturally!) tell others the simple good news of Jesus: who He is and what He has done for us.

————

## Points to ponder

- Who in your life needs to hear about Jesus? Pray consistently for them and ask the Holy Spirit to show you ways to reach them.
- Are there events you could bring your friends to in the near future? Ask God to give you boldness and confidence to invite them.
- One of the best ways to share your faith with others is by using a simple picture such as the bridge illustration. With God on one side and mankind on the other side, separated by a gulf of sin, Christ is the bridge between God and mankind, and each of us has a choice to cross that bridge.

————

## Prayer

*Lord, thank You for the reality and wonder of the good news. Forgive me for my lack of passion or timidity in telling others. Please empower me and give me boldness and joy to share the good news of what You have done in my life and what You have done to save the world. Amen!*

# 03

## WHEN JESUS COMES IN THE MIDST

John 20:19–31

# 15 NEW PEACE

## John 20:19

I wonder what expectations you have if and when you come to a church worship service or meet in a small group? Well, according to Matthew 18:20, every time Christians meet together in the name of Jesus, there is the promise that the risen Christ will be present in their midst. During the 40 days after the resurrection this happened as Jesus physically appeared to His disciples in His resurrection body. Since the ascension (see Days 35 and 40) and the Day of Pentecost (Acts 2), Jesus is present among His people, in and through the person of the Holy Spirit. When He comes, one of the primary hallmarks of His presence is His peace.

This week we are going look at how Jesus came into the midst of two small group meetings: the first was to ten of the disciples on Easter Sunday evening; the second was a week later with all 11 disciples, including Thomas. While there are aspects of those encounters that were unique to the 40 days, there is much to inspire our sense of expectancy as Christ presents Himself in our midst today.

The first appearance was on Easter Sunday evening. Despite the evidence of the empty tomb, and news of at least three separate appearances during the day – to Mary and the women, to the Emmaus disciples and to Peter – the disciples as a group are still fearful enough to be hiding behind closed doors. Then Jesus came in their midst: 'On the evening of that first day of the week, when the disciples were together, with the doors locked for fear of the Jewish leaders, Jesus came and stood among them and said, "Peace be with you!"' (John 20:19).

What are we to make of Jesus' appearance in a room with locked doors? Some commentators suggest that, as with Peter in prison (Acts 12), the doors may have miraculously opened.

However, the absence of any such reference here makes this unlikely. So, we are left with the surprising but significant conclusion that Jesus simply 'appeared' in the room in a real physical body (it could be touched), yet one which was somehow not restricted by what we consider to be the laws of physics (it could pass through grave clothes and closed doors).

When Jesus appeared the first thing that He did was to declare: 'Peace be with you!' and then a short while later, to repeat the blessing (John 20:19, 21).[15]

I love this! At one level, Jesus is simply giving the standard greeting of the time 'shalom aleichem' (peace be upon you). At a deeper level He is saying something of extraordinary and universal significance. To His defeated, demoralised, depressed and discouraged disciples, probably weary and running on empty, He said: 'Peace be upon you. It's going to be OK. I've got everything under control!' I also love this because of what He didn't say. He didn't criticise them for abandoning Him on the cross. He didn't rebuke them. He didn't scold them. That's good news! If you don't understand anything else, I want you to get this right now. Nobody understands how you feel as much as Jesus Christ does. God understands how you feel more than *you* understand how you feel, and He wants to come to you and encourage you, even if you feel you have let Him down.

Furthermore, this word 'peace' is more than just a word of reassurance: 'don't be troubled or anxious'. It's more than just a nice feeling of tranquillity. Rather, this double proclamation of *peace* is greatly significant. It carries with it the full richness of the Hebrew *shalom*, meaning wholeness, wellbeing and the idea that life can be lived as God intended.

Fundamental to biblical shalom is what we would call *eternal peace* – or peace with God. Because of mankind's rebellion against the Creator, we have all fallen short of His standards and are under His judgment (Rom. 3:23; Heb. 9:27). That is fundamentally why Christ came to die in our place and bring 'peace' and reconciliation between us and God. In Romans 5:1 Paul says that 'since we have been justified through faith, we have peace with God through our Lord Jesus Christ'. Because Jesus was raised from the dead, we know that the price for our sins on the cross was paid – it was finished, *paid in full* – and therefore we can eternally be at peace with God.

Once we know this eternal peace, we receive an *internal peace* – where we can be at peace with ourselves. Inner peace is something we all desire, but it often proves elusive. There is an extraordinary restlessness within human beings, which makes us unable to experience peace. The great French thinker Blaise Pascal said this: 'All of humanity's problems stem from man's inability to sit quietly in a room alone.' In other words, our lack of peace drives us to greed, selfishness, materialism, sexual immorality, foolish ambition and so on. We search for peace in all the wrong places. The peace that Jesus came to bring is a peace that is independent of circumstances. The world's peace can only be produced by externals such as prosperity and tranquility; God's peace can be felt in the heat of battle or on the way to the operating theatre. It is a standard view in Christianity that our failure to have peace with ourselves and peace with our fellow humans is ultimately the outworking of that greatest of all problems: a lack of peace with God. However, when we know that we have peace with God, and trust Him, choosing not to worry and pray, we can enjoy, 'the peace of God, which transcends all understanding' (Phil. 4:7).

Then when we are enjoying eternal and internal peace we can start manifesting an *external peace* – a peace in our own relationships with others. Moreover we can be those who carry the 'gospel of peace' (Eph. 6:15) into a lost and fractured world.

All of this and more was wrapped up in the declaration of that marvellous word, 'shalom', when the risen Jesus appeared to His disciples on that first Easter evening. The good news is that we too can expect Christ to come into our midst bringing this shalom – helping us to live the life that He intended. In this age we enjoy the foretaste; in the age to come the fullness!

## Points to ponder

- In your experience, how do people imagine that they will find peace?
- What does it mean for you to be at peace with God? How will that affect the way you live today?
- Becoming a Christian means knowing God as Father. How does our new status as children of God help bring peace to our lives?
- Imagine someone who truly was at peace with God. What do you think would strike you about the way they talked and behaved?
- How well do you manifest peace to those around you?

## Prayer

*Jesus, Prince of peace, I thank You for paying for my sins in full so that I can be eternally at peace with God. Lord, it is life's biggest privilege to be in relationship with You, knowing that when You see me, You see me clean and blameless, without blemish or sin. I receive this wonderful truth again. Holy Spirit, continue to remind me of this when circumstances around me try to steal my peace and when people around me are living in anxiety. You are my rock, fortress and deliverer, in whom I take refuge (Psa. 18:2). Help me to bring peace to those around me. In Jesus' name. Amen.*

# NEW HOPE

## John 20:20; Luke 24:36–43

Have you ever experienced a time when you felt like all hope was gone? If so, then you will be able to identify to some degree with how the disciples must have felt on Good Friday. One of the major impacts of Jesus' death on the disciples was, as we have already seen, the crushing of hope. As Jesus was cruelly crucified, so too were their hopes for the future in Him as the Messiah. That is until Easter Sunday, when death itself was defeated! One of the primary effects of the resurrection, then and now, is the restoration of hope. This is based not on some kind of vaguely optimistic 'hope so' that things will get better, but rather a hope that is certain, based on the 'solid' evidence that Jesus has been physically raised from the dead.

The reality of the physical resurrection of Jesus is at the very heart of the new hope that is at the centre of the Christian message. Hence, after having declared 'Peace', Jesus sought to give the startled disciples clear and convincing proofs that He was really, physically alive. We read in John's account how 'he showed them his hands and side' (John 20:20). What is Jesus doing? In effect, He is revealing His true identity. In Luke's parallel account this comes out even more clearly. The disciples are frightened, thinking He's a ghost (literally a 'phantom'), to which Jesus replies: 'Look at my hands and my feet. It is I myself! Touch me and see; a ghost does not have flesh and bones, as you see I have' (Luke 24:39). He is saying, 'It's me. See the nail prints here. This was the price I paid for you to be free. But it's really me. You're not looking at a ghost. You're not looking at a vision. You're not dreaming. Touch me. It's really me. I'm back.' When they still struggle to believe, Jesus asked for 'a piece of broiled fish, and he took it and ate it in their presence' (Luke 24:42–43).

How wonderfully real and tangible: 'You think I'm a ghost! Give me a piece of fish to eat!'

The implications stretch way beyond this encounter to the very end of history. A man who was clearly dead for three days; that same man has overcome death and is really alive. Yet this same man was somehow different – able just to 'appear' in the room. Here is what is so significant: God did not do away with the old body of Jesus and create a brand new one. Instead, He took the recognisable physical body that was nailed to the cross and had a spear thrust in its side, raised it back to life and clothed it with immortality, so that it was somehow different, unlimited, and more glorious. Jesus' resurrection was His vindication, as God's true King, God's true prophet and God's perfect priest. Yet it is more than that: it also looks forward to the end of the age with Jesus as the prototype of our own resurrection. As He rose in a body that was both a continuation of His earthly body and also a transformed heavenly one, so we will rise in a similar way.

For those who are 'in Christ' at His second appearing at the end of history, there is a certain, glorious hope. The future resurrection makes sense of all the pains and labours of this present life. Let me illustrate:

If two women were given the same offer of a job that was very tedious, that would require 80 hours a week, would last for a whole year and would include no holidays, and yet one had the promise of a pay cheque at the end of £15,000 and the other of £15,000,000 do you think their attitude would be different? The first would probably live that year disgruntled, bored, maybe even resentful and depressed. The second one would be buoyed up through the long hours, tedium and tiredness, because she would be thinking about how she could spend her millions.

The great news of Christianity is that our hope is far greater than money. Whatever challenges and trials we face in this life, we can be assured that there is a glorious hope that will far outweigh all of this. Because Jesus conquered death, and is alive, we no longer need to fear death. As He really is alive in a glorified physical body, we can be assured that we will receive new bodies, never subject to death, ageing, sickness, pain or tiredness.

Moreover, we will live eternally in God's presence and kingdom in a new heaven, on a transformed earth.

The disciples on that first Easter Sunday wouldn't, of course, have grasped all this. But one thing they did know: the Jesus whom they had followed as Messiah, whom they had thought was dead and buried, had in fact defeated death and was standing alive in their midst. Over the next 40 days they became more and more convinced that not only was this true but that it changed everything – not just for the present, but for the future. After they received the Spirit on the Day of Pentecost, the full importance of the event started to dawn on them. The first church leaders were led and guided by the Holy Spirit to write accounts of the story of Jesus and letters that expressed God's truth to His people, which together make up what we know as the New Testament. Even a cursory reading of these letters and the final book of Revelation highlight that hope for the future, based on the reality of the physical resurrection of Jesus. Such hope transformed their view of their present struggles and gave them tremendous confidence in a future with Jesus alive, reigning and returning one day! One of the tremendous weaknesses of atheism is its inability to deal with death. Death destroys everything: because of death even the most successful human life is ultimately a tragedy. But Jesus' resurrection makes everything worthwhile.

---

## Points to ponder

- In a world that believes that death has the last word can anything be a truly lasting success?
- How does the idea of resurrection transform our disappointments over what we might have failed to achieve?
- How hopeful do you feel about your future? Do you need to ask God to heal any sense you have had of feeling hopeless? Take some time to reflect on the great future that is available because of Jesus and His resurrection.

## Prayer

*Thank You God for the glorious hope that I have in You. As strange as it may seem now, Your Word says that one day, there will be 'a new heaven and a new earth' (Rev. 21:1). Whatever that may mean, I know that this is something to look forward to! I offer up my life to you afresh. Despite what I may face today, I cling to the hope that one day there will be no death, crying, mourning or pain (Rev. 21:4). May I be someone who increasingly lives with eternity in mind. Amen.*

# Day

# 17 NEW JOY

## John 20:20

As I wrote yesterday about the new hope that we have in Jesus, I found myself being filled with new joy! It is no surprise that once the disciples had grasped that this person in their midst was Jesus, alive from the dead, they were indeed filled with new joy. Hence we read: 'The disciples were overjoyed when they saw the Lord' (John 20:20).

It has been said that when the translators came to translate the Bible for the Inuit peoples of the Arctic and they got to this particular verse in John 20, they were stumped. The Inuit language doesn't deal in abstract concepts so they struggled to find a verb that conveys the idea of being 'overjoyed'. Then one of the translators hit on a perfect solution. He noticed how close the bond was between the Inuit men and their husky dogs and how when the men got up in the morning to let out the huskies the dogs were so overjoyed that they wagged their tails with great delight. The translator suggested that they used this idea in the Inuit translation of the Bible. So, the translation reads: 'The disciples wagged their tails when they saw the Lord.' In one West African language the word 'joy' means, literally, 'song in the body' which is nearly as good as wagging your tail! I'm not suggesting we change our English Bibles to suit, but it does help convey the tremendous sense of how having seen the risen Lord, the disciples experienced a *breakout* of joy. Their grief and sense of defeat had turned into overwhelming joy. In the words of one scholar: 'Joy is the basic mood of Easter.'[16]

It is important to realise the 'joy' experienced here, and spoken of throughout the Bible, is essentially different from how we normally view 'happiness' today. There is nothing wrong with happiness: it's great to be happy! The problem is that happiness is essentially based on our mood and circumstances. Our state of happiness can go up and down, based on everything from the weather, through to whether we have had enough sleep. Biblical joy, which affects our happiness, is, however, dependent on something much deeper. It is based on a revelation of Jesus, and comes from a relationship with the 'joyful' Holy Spirit (Rom. 14:17; Gal. 5:22). It is worth adding that although we tend to think of joy as being something that is exuberant and expressed with words and gestures, there can also be a quiet joy.

The joy of the Lord brings tremendous benefits to our lives. In Nehemiah 8:10, we discover that 'the joy of the Lord is your strength'. Elsewhere in Proverbs 17:22, we see that 'A joyful heart is good medicine, but a crushed spirit dries up the bones' (ESV). In other words joy in our hearts can affect every area of our lives, bringing strength and health to our whole being.

This joy is something that we can experience in our own individual walk. When I first became a Christian I experienced a tremendous sense of joy, and as I continue to walk with the Holy Spirit, I enjoy the joy of the Lord. Countless times I have found my joy being rekindled as I enter the 'house of prayer' (Isa. 56:7), and as I read and reflect on the Word of God. Like the prophet Jeremiah I can say: 'When your words came, I ate them; they were my joy and my heart's delight' (Jer. 15:16).

In the context of Easter, it is important to remember that it was the presence of the risen Jesus in the midst of His disciples that caused them to overflow with joy. As we gather together in meetings small and large, it is the remembrance of Jesus, crucified and risen, and the reality of His presence that changes the atmosphere around us.

May you know a new joy today!

## Points to ponder

- How much pleasure do you feel when you spend time with the Lord?
- Look back at the difference between joy and happiness. When was the last time you experienced true joy? Ask the Spirit to fill you and keep on filling you with His joy.
- It has been said that people are either thermometers or thermostats; they either do nothing more than register the temperature of what is around them, or they seek to control it. In the area of joy, why not deliberately choose to be a thermostat, bringing joy into every place you go, consciously welcoming the presence of Jesus in those situations.

## Prayer

*Lord, Your Word says that joy is a 'fruit of the Spirit' (Gal. 5:22). I want to experience Your joy in greater measures. Holy Spirit, fill me to overflowing so that I may experience the true joy that runs deep; joy that is not swayed by the circumstances of life; joy that causes my heart to rejoice no matter what I am facing. Today, I will rejoice and be glad in You (Psa. 9:2). Amen.*

# NEW PURPOSE

## John 20:21

Unbeknown to many in our world today, living for ourselves in the total pursuit of 'success' is *not* the ultimate goal of life. Rather, we are called to live 'beyond ourselves' and to live lives of great 'significance', in pursuit of God's agenda. Sadly, for many people, life is without an ultimate purpose: we are born, we live, we eat, we sleep, we shop and then we die! Encountering the risen Christ changes all this.

Significantly, when Jesus appeared amongst His disciples on that first Easter Sunday evening, He not only blessed them and changed their world (bringing new peace, hope and joy to them), but He commissioned them to go and be a blessing, and change the world in His name. The pattern is the same for us today.

This is so important for us to realise. It is wonderful to have your own life changed. It is even more amazing to then spend the rest of your life working in partnership with the living God to see other people's lives changed.

This grand purpose is set out by Jesus in what is sometimes called the Johannine Commission: 'As the Father has sent me, I am sending you' (John 20:21). This is the grandest possible purpose. The language here is striking: the mission of Jesus and the mission of the disciples are depicted here as *one* mission. This is hugely important. Just as the Father has sent Jesus, so Jesus now sends His people – to bring the good news of His saving, redeeming and restoring love to a fallen world.

What amazing grace! To a group of disciples who had failed Him, and deserted Him in His hour of trial, Jesus comes and reveals God's plan: 'you're going to help me continue my mission – to restore and redeem the whole world'. What's even more amazing is that they did! This small group of previously frightened disciples took the good news of Jesus' resurrection out into the city. Within decades, the news was all over the Middle East; within 300 years it had taken over the Roman Empire, and today, one-third of the world's population claim to be Christians. It was the biggest task ever given.

We now have the privilege of continuing that same mission today. God has a far greater plan for us than simply living for ourselves. Rather we are called to live *beyond* ourselves. It is so important that we don't end up missing this.

A rich man was determined to give his mother a birthday present that would outshine all others. He read of a bird that had a vocabulary of 4,000 words, could speak in numerous languages and sing 3 operatic arias. He immediately bought the bird for £50,000 and had it delivered to his mother. The next day he phoned to see if she had received the bird. 'What did you think of the bird?' he asked. She replied, 'It was delicious.' (It was a total waste of the bird's potential!)

Let's make sure that we don't end up living *below* God's plan for us. You may have messed up in life, but God's plan for your life is greater than any plan you could ever think of for yourself. You were made for more than success. God made you for significance. You're made for more than money; you're made for meaning. You're made for more than possessions; you're made for a purpose. All the possessions in the world will not compensate for a lack of purpose in your life. Many books and films today involve heroes who are called to save the world. But this is just fantasy. As Christians, we really are called to be world-changers! This involves both sharing the good news so that people are changed, and bringing God's kingdom rules into the world by tackling issues like social injustice.

## Points to ponder

- To what extent can you say that you live 'beyond yourself' on a daily basis?
- Where do you believe that the Lord has sent or is going to send you? Perhaps it's a certain city or country. Maybe He has called you to a certain people group. Take some time to bring this before the Lord and ask that He will equip you afresh for the mission.
- Most of us are 'sent' to our immediate workplace, neighbourhood and family and this is where we are to live out our call to mission in word and deed (more on Day 31).
- How passionate are you for this aspect of mission? Do you need to ask God to give you a fresh heart of compassion and love for those immediately around you who do not yet know God?

## Prayer

*Lord, use me for Your glory. May I increasingly be a generous giver of my time, resources and talent so that Your kingdom may come and Your will be done (Matt. 6:10). By Your Spirit, guide me to each place where You have called me to be a blessing. Help me to bring Your joy to those who need it and Your justice to those who are being unfairly treated. Equip me, anoint me and give me the courage and energy to fulfill the purpose You have for me. Let me be Your hands and feet. Here I am. Send me (Isa. 6:8)! Amen.*

# NEW POWER AND AUTHORITY

## John 20:22–23

On a couple of occasions I have been silly enough to drive my car without enough fuel. The result? It stopped! Potentially more serious though, was the time I filled my wife's diesel car with petrol. As I drove off from the forecourt I realised that something was amiss!

Just as we need enough of the right kind of fuel to drive our cars, so we need the right kind of power to fulfill our purpose in life. Yesterday we saw that we are called to a grand purpose: to continue the mission of God. At first, this can seem somewhat intimidating, until we realise that God has given us all the power and authority we need to carry on that commission. We see this in Jesus' encounter with His disciples. Having commissioned them, He immediately empowered them: 'And with that he breathed on them and said, "Receive the Holy Spirit"' (John 20:22).

This alludes to two Old Testament instances in which humans were God-breathed to life. The first is that of creation, when in Genesis 2, God breathed into Adam and He became a living being. The second is found in Ezekiel 37 where God is seen to symbolically breathe into His people, and they come to life and stand up 'as a vast army'. Not an army of 'hate' and 'destruction' but an army filled with His very presence and life, and empowered to bring new life to the world!

So, in summary, what does Jesus breathing on the disciples mean for them and for us? It demonstrates that the only way we can receive a new life is by receiving the Holy Spirit, and if we are going to live in the new heavens and the new earth, we have to be made a *new creation*. Now raised from the dead, Jesus breathes the Spirit into His followers so that they not only come alive with the life of

God, but also so that they are empowered to go and bring new life to the world around them. For us this means that as we go out into the world to fulfill His agenda of gospel transformation, we are not on our own. Rather, we have Jesus' very personal empowering, in the person of the Holy Spirit. In the Spirit, we have all the love, power and wisdom we are ever going to need to enable us to see God's purposes affected on the earth.

Having given the disciples the promise of new life and power through the Holy Spirit, He now gives them a new message and the authority to proclaim it: 'If you forgive anyone's sins, their sins are forgiven; if you do not forgive them, they are not forgiven' (John 20:23). Jesus is not saying that it is up to us to take the place of God in saying who is to be forgiven and who isn't. No, this rather strange statement is best understood in the broader context of our mission to proclaim the good news. This comes out much more clearly in Luke 24. Jesus is showing the disciples how He is the fulfillment of the Old Testament, and how: 'the Messiah will suffer and rise from the dead on the third day, and repentance for the forgiveness of sins will be preached in his name to all nations, beginning at Jerusalem. You are witnesses of these things' (Luke 24:46-48). Notice that the role of the church is not focused on deciding who will and who won't be forgiven, but rather to go and preach the gospel, at the heart of which is the promise of 'forgiveness of sins'. This is good news! To those who repent and believe the gospel, there is the offer of forgiveness. Yet for those who reject the good news, they will stay in their sins and therefore will not be forgiven: a fact which only highlights the importance of the task ahead.

This giving of authority to proclaim the good news of forgiveness must stay at the heart of our message of transformation. While it is vital that we live good lives, and do good works, ultimately, our message needs to be proclaimed in such a way that people are given the opportunity to receive the forgiveness of sins, without which there is no salvation and no eternal life.

As we conclude our thoughts on this Easter Sunday evening meeting, it is important that we step back and reflect. The message is not one of simply saying: make it your goal to receive the gifts of new peace, hope, joy, purpose, power and authority. Rather, the call is to welcome Jesus the giver, and He will fill you with these. As we go into our daily lives, let's expect new encounters with Jesus; life-changing encounters for ourselves and for all who come into our midst!

## Points to ponder

- How does it feel to be part of an army of God followers?
- Are there areas of your life that feel dead right now? Why not invite the Holy Spirit to fill you with His refreshing presence and power?
- Which 'fruit of the Spirit' (Gal. 5:22–23) would you like more of in your own life?

## Prayer

*Father, thank You for the wonderful gift of Your Holy Spirit. This day, I open up my life to You afresh and invite You to fill me again. Reproduce in me the fruit of the Spirit so that I might reflect Your character everywhere I go today. Clothe me with power from on high and grant me opportunities to speak out about You and to demonstrate the truth of the resurrection. In the mighty name of Jesus. Amen.*

# Day

# 20 'DOUBTING THOMAS'

## John 20:24–25

All of us at some time in our lives have struggled with matters of faith. Today, we centre our attention on the story of one man, famously known as 'Doubting Thomas'. 'Now Thomas (also known as Didymus), one of the Twelve, was not with the disciples when Jesus came. So the other disciples told him, "We have seen the Lord!" But he said to them, "Unless I see the nail marks in his hands and put my finger where the nails were, and put my hand into his side, I will not believe"' (John 20:24–25).

Having been present with Jesus for much of His ministry, Thomas missed *the* moment when Jesus had presented Himself alive, proclaimed peace and gave the others their world-changing assignment. Thomas might have felt guilty about missing the first appearance, he might have felt devastated at not being there or he might even have felt that he had been excluded from that blessing by God.

Whatever the reasons for his absence, Thomas makes one thing quite clear: he was not going to believe in the resurrection based on what the others had told him. No, he required first-hand, visible proof or he would 'not believe'. People sometimes say, 'That's my problem! If I could see and touch God, I would believe in him.' Even if you are a follower of Jesus, you may simply have honest questions rising from your experiences of life.

There is nothing wrong with honest questions as long as they don't descend into unbelief or cynicism. It's like the difference between travelling through a tunnel and going down a cave. Questions that are genuinely honest and explorative are tunnel questions – light will come.

The deeper you go through a tunnel, the nearer the light you get. Questions that are cynical, destructive or negative, however, are like going into a cave. The deeper you go down, the darker it gets. Cave questions are not so much trying to find answers to difficult questions, but rather an attempt to hide from the truth.

Thomas was a genuine questioner. We know that because out of His questions came great revelation. This had already happened once before. In John 14, Jesus was reassuring His disciples that He was going ahead of them to prepare a place for them and then added, 'You know the way to the place where I am going.' To this Thomas replied, 'Lord we don't know where you are going, so how can we know the way?' (John 14:4–5). This is an honest question that led to Jesus making one of His most important self-declarations: 'I am the way and the truth and the life. No one comes to the Father except through me' (John 14:6).

## Points to ponder

- Have there been any times recently where you felt you missed out on an opportunity to encounter Christ? Be encouraged – He wants to meet with you again.
- Think about any questions you have about faith. Are they 'tunnel' questions or 'cave' questions? Have you ever spoken with God about them? Sometimes, the very act of praying about them brings a sense of supernatural peace.

## Prayer

*God, I thank You for always being gracious and patient with me, even in my moments of unbelief. I bring before You every question and doubt that I am holding in my heart about You, about faith or about the future. I offer up every circumstance in my life that has perplexed me and has caused me to question Your goodness and sovereignty. I ask that Your peace, that surpasses all understanding, would guard my heart and my mind today (Phil. 4:7). Amen.*

# TWO TYPES OF FAITH

## John 20:26–29

There are essentially two types of faith. There is the Thomas-like faith which needs to see something before it can believe, and there is true biblical faith that pleases God, which believes *before* it sees. Both types of faith are in evidence in our verses today: 'A week later his disciples were in the house again, and Thomas was with them. Though the doors were locked, Jesus came and stood among them and said, "Peace be with you!" Then he said to Thomas, "Put your finger here; see my hands. Reach out your hand and put it into my side. Stop doubting and believe." Thomas said to him, "My Lord and my God!" Then Jesus told him, "Because you have seen me, you have believed; blessed are those who have not seen and yet have believed"' (John 20:26–29).

It is worth pausing just to emphasise that Jesus doesn't appear when Thomas is on his own, but rather when the disciples are gathered together again. This fact that almost all the described resurrection appearances were to groups of people both counter the suggestion that they were hallucinations and also remind us that our experience of Christ is to be shared.

As Jesus appeared to the group a second time, He makes ministering to Thomas a priority. Having clearly 'overheard' Thomas' comments concerning his need to 'see' and 'touch', Jesus very specifically invites him to touch the physical wounds from His crucifixion: His pierced hands and the open wound in His side where the spear had penetrated His flesh. Can you imagine the tension in the room?

In 1602 the artist Caravaggio painted *The Incredulity of Saint Thomas*, a powerful painting in which he tries to imagine the scene and has the hand of Christ guiding the hand of Thomas into the wound on his side. There is however, no evidence here that Thomas actually touched Jesus – he didn't need to. This was clearly the same Jesus who had been crucified and now, only ten days later, was standing before Thomas alive and well! As Thomas looks at Jesus, his questions fall like scales from his eyes and his doubt turns to faith, as he responds dramatically: 'My Lord and my God!' This is a wonderful moment when from the furnace of doubt emerges one of the finest confessions of faith in Jesus found in the New Testament.

This declaration of Jesus as his Lord (Greek *Kyrios*) and God (Greek *Theos*) provides a literary link with the references to Jesus as God in John's prologue (1:1,18), and is one of the strongest texts in the New Testament for the divinity of Christ. It was not, as some cults have tried to argue, an exclamation of astonishment, but a declaration of worship, directed personally to Jesus. In the context of Jewish monotheism, it is striking that Jesus doesn't attempt to correct Thomas, but rather receives his worship. For Thomas, this was clearly a moment of profound importance; so much so that according to Early Church history he went on to take the gospel to India, eventually being martyred for his faith in the risen Christ.

Thomas did believe, but his 'faith' was based on 'seeing'. However, Jesus announces that a new age was about to dawn when people would believe without seeing (John 20:29). Peter, who would have been in the room at that moment, summarises the joy available to all who exercise this kind of faith: 'Though you have not seen him [Jesus], you love him; and even though you do not see him now, you believe in him and are filled with an inexpressible and glorious joy, for you are receiving the end result of your faith, the salvation of your souls' (1 Peter 1:8-9).

So, be encouraged! To believe without seeing is the kind of faith that truly pleases God. Such faith brings joy today and great hope for tomorrow!

## Points to ponder

- Were Thomas' doubts justified? Are any doubts justified?
- If someone were to ask you: 'How can you believe in a God you cannot see?' what would your response be?
- Today, are you filled with an 'inexpressible and glorious joy' because of your belief in Jesus?
- Do you in any way need to hear Jesus saying to you, just as He did to Thomas: 'Stop doubting and believe'?

## Prayer

*Lord, You are completely trustworthy. I do believe in You; help me overcome my unbelief (Mark 9:24). Amen!*

WEEK

# 04

## OVERCOMING FAILURE

John 21:1–22

# YOUR FUTURE IS GREATER THAN YOUR FAILURE

## John 21:1,14

This week we are going to be looking at the important subject of overcoming failure. All of us struggle in life and have failed in various ways. Some of us are still living in the consequences of that failure – and have wondered whether we can ever get beyond it. Well I've got some great news for you: your future is greater than your failure; the call is greater than the fall!

History is full of people who have overcome failure:

He did not speak until he was four and did not read until he was seven, causing his teachers and parents to think he had learning difficulties, was slow and anti-social. Eventually, he was expelled from school and was refused admittance to the Zurich Polytechnic School. It might have taken him a bit longer, but most people would agree that he caught on pretty well in the end, winning the Nobel Prize and changing the face of modern physics … his name? Albert Einstein!

Today, we are going to be studying another stunning example of overcoming failure. The man's name is Simon Peter. He grew up around the Sea of Galilee, became a fisherman and was first introduced to Jesus by his brother Andrew. At that moment, Jesus gave him the nickname 'Peter', which means rock or stone (John 1:41–42). Throughout the rest of Jesus' earthly ministry Peter was not only one of the Twelve, and part of what seemed like an inner core of three (along with James and John), but in many ways he was the leader or spokesperson for the group. He had some great high points: such as when he made the famous declaration concerning Jesus as 'the Messiah, the Son of the living God' which resulted in Jesus saying: 'Now I say to you that you are Peter (which means 'rock'), and upon this rock I will build my church' (Matt. 16:15–18, NLT). Yet he also displayed a particular proficiency for saying the wrong thing at the wrong time, and immediately after this great confession was rebuked by Jesus for his misunderstanding of Jesus' calling to go to the cross (Matt. 16:22–23). His life descended to a particular low point in the events leading up to the crucifixion, most notably when he denied Jesus three times. Yet Jesus had great plans for Peter. He personally appeared to him some time on Easter Day (Luke 24:34; 1 Cor. 15:5). Then He appeared to him again on the evening of that same day, and then a week later in the meeting with Thomas. However, it seems that Peter needed further restoration. Hence, in John 21 we see Jesus appearing again to seven of the disciples on the shore of Galilee, with Peter the main focus of His attention. Oh, the loving persistence and complete thoroughness of the grace of God!

This week we will look at the two main incidents concerning the miraculous catch of fish, followed by the breakfast by the sea (John 21:1–14), and Jesus' restoration and re-commissioning of Peter (John 21:15–22). This wonderful chapter is one of the most encouraging and hope-filled in the whole of Scripture. It highlights just how willing and able Jesus is to enable us to overcome failure: by helping us in our present struggles and healing us of our past sins and disappointments.

So great was the effect of this seashore encounter (along with the cumulative effects of the previous appearances) that shortly thereafter Peter the failed fisherman, who fearfully denied Jesus at his hour of greatest trial, boldly stood up before a huge crowd in Jerusalem, and preached that the crucified Jesus was now risen and the Lord who was to be worshipped. This resulted in 3,000 people coming to faith and being added to the new church. From this breakthrough moment on the Day of Pentecost, Peter went on to become the 'rock' and is rightly honoured, alongside Paul, as one of the two key foundational leaders of the Church of Jesus Christ.

Maybe as you are reading this you are still struggling with the crippling effects of failure, and are wondering whether you can ever succeed again. This week, starting today, you can take heart!

No matter how much you feel you are failing or have failed, Jesus is alive and wanting to help you and restore you. Let me remind you again: with God, your future is greater than your failure; the call is greater than the fall!

___

## Points to ponder

- What is your initial reaction when you experience failure?
- Have you ever let your failures define you? (Al Gore once introduced himself in this way: 'I'm Al Gore, I used to be the next president of the United States of America.')
- Do you know what the 'call' of God is on your life? Remind yourself of this. If you are not yet sure, invite the Lord to begin or continue to make this clear to you, in His timings and in His way.

___

## Prayer

*Lord, I believe that You are my biggest advocate. I thank You that You delight in me every day. I take hold of the truth that my identity lies in Christ, not on my achievements or performance in life. Thank You for the truth that my past failures do not have to determine my future. Cleanse and heal me from any place where past failure is trying to cling onto me. Wipe away my guilt and strengthen my heart. Show me more clearly what You want me to do. Amen.*

# JESUS HELPS US IN OUR PRESENT STRUGGLES

---

## John 21:1–4

All of us face struggles and challenges in life. Right now you may have no more than a vague sense that you need a miraculous intervention from God in your life; or you may have reached a definite barrier that you need to overcome but can't; or you may just be quietly certain that you have reached rock bottom. The great news from John 21 is that Jesus is alive and present by His Spirit, and He is both willing and able to help.

This week's encounter took place in Galilee, with Jesus this time appearing to seven of the disciples: 'Afterwards Jesus appeared again to his disciples, by the Sea of Galilee. It happened this way: Simon Peter, Thomas (also known as Didymus), Nathaniel from Cana in Galilee, the sons of Zebedee, and two other disciples were together. "I'm going out to fish," Simon Peter told them, and they said, "We'll go with you." So they went out and got into the boat, but that night they caught nothing' (John 21:1–3).

Peter is often criticised here for going fishing – as if somehow he was running from the call of God on his life. However, it is more likely that he is simply filling the time (waiting for Jesus to appear to them at Galilee as he had promised). On the most basic level, he may just have been going out to earn some money; even the most godly still need to eat![17] He is not doing something that is overtly wrong – just doing a normal 'human' thing. Yet in spite of doing what he was trained to do, and fishing when he should have done (at night), he and the others still caught nothing. This is the key point. Their struggle, failure and subsequent frustration, like ours, is part of being human in a fallen world, living with limitations and frustrations. Yet, into this situation of struggle and failure Jesus comes on the scene: 'Early in the morning,

Jesus stood on the shore, but the disciples did not realise that it was Jesus' (John 21:4). This has echoes of the Emmaus appearance – Jesus is present to help, but initially the disciples don't recognise Him (again, the suggestion is that somehow He looked different in his post-resurrection state). But the point is that Jesus was right there watching and waiting to help – not watching in order to criticise!

This story of failed fishing has two possible applications:

1) Fishing without success can represent our daily lives – our work, our families, our relationships – and our need of Jesus to help us;

2) Fishing can represent the mission of the Church. In Ezekiel 47, for example, the fish in the river of God were symbolic of people, and when Jesus first called the disciples He talked about being 'fishers of people' (Matt. 4:19).

Whether we look at our daily lives or apply it to our mission as the people of God, the point seems clear: we are not supposed to carry on without His help. The wonderful news of this story is that we don't need to: Jesus is present with us, ready to assist.

So, if you are currently in a situation where you are experiencing failure, or just feel stuck and need a breakthrough, take the opportunity this week to turn to Jesus. He really is alive and is both willing and able to help, no matter how hopeless the situation may seem.

## Points to ponder

- Are there any parts of your life where you feel like you have nothing to show but empty nets? Think about your workplace, family and relationships; how fruitful are they at the moment?
- In what areas of your life would you like to see more 'fish'? Are you playing your part in seeing people won to Jesus? If not, invite Jesus to teach you how to become more effective in winning people to Him.
- Fishing in Bible times was not an individual activity but a group one. With whom are you working in terms of 'fishing' together? If you are in a church small group encourage each other to pray and work together to see people won to Christ. Go 'fishing' together!

## Prayer

*Lord, I thank You today for Your goodness and faithfulness. You are gracious, compassionate, slow to anger and rich in love (Psa. 145:8). I approach You boldly, knowing that You have good plans for me. I lift up every area of my life that is currently lacking 'fish'. Show me if there is anything I can do to be more productive and fruitful. In Jesus' name. Amen.*

# Day
## 24

# RESPOND TO THE HELPER

## John 21:5-6

We saw yesterday a picture of Jesus watching and waiting to intervene on the seashore, with the disciples out there on a failed fishing expedition. Yet Jesus doesn't stand idly by, but initiates the first conversation: 'He called out to them, "Friends, haven't you any fish?" "No", they answered' (John 21:5). Notice, too, His heart for them – He addresses them as 'children' or 'lads' – a term of great endearment and affection, which reveals the Father-heart of God. This is not a God who remains distant, formal and aloof, but a God who comes close, who is personal and ready to help. Needless to say, Jesus doesn't ask the question about the catch because He doesn't know the answer. Rather, He is simply engaging with them. God never asks a question to which He doesn't know the answer.

The disciples answer with a simple and honest response. They don't seem to resent this question as an intrusion or an insult – they don't try and deny or hide the problem, by saying, 'No, we're fine thanks, we can manage!' Moreover, there is no suggestion throughout the rest of the passage that the disciples resent His intervention, however awkward or challenging it may be. Here's a primary key if we want Jesus to help us in our present struggles – we must *welcome* His intervention.

Yet it is not enough simply to welcome Christ's presence into our situation, but rather we must, like these disciples, respond and do what He tells us to do: 'He said, "Throw your net on the right side of the boat and you will find some." When they did, they were unable to haul the net in because of the large number of fish' (John 21:6). I love this! We don't know whether this instruction was based on a word of knowledge concerning the whereabouts of the fish, or whether He commanded and they obeyed Him! Either way, we can be assured that Jesus the risen one and the Creator Himself has all the knowledge and power that we will ever need. He knows more about the fish than the fishermen! He knows more about accountancy than the accountant, more about business than the businessman, more about parenting than parents, more about teaching than teachers, and more about reaching people with the gospel than we do. Moreover, He is not just able; He is willing, alive and present with us by His Spirit, ready to help us in every area of our life and ministry. There is never a situation or circumstance where He is not there – even if we don't recognise Him fully.

The key is to obey when He speaks. In the ESV translation, Jesus' instruction is translated in a simple phrase: 'cast the net', and of the disciples it says: 'so they cast it'. The unquestioning obedience of the disciples is worth noting. These were experienced fishermen who had been fishing all night (the optimum time), and yet here they are obeying the voice of a stranger. There must have been something compelling about the way He said it that overcame their reluctance.

Many Christian leaders throughout the centuries have pointed out the necessity of listening to the quiet whispers of God. The more we walk with the Spirit, and immerse ourselves in the Word, the more sensitive we can become to these promptings. Sometimes the Lord speaks to us as we are reading the Bible, sometimes as we are listening to someone preach, sometimes we can hear a confirming word to us through a prophecy, sometimes through a night dream. However, very often there is the guidance that comes from an inner witness or a 'still, small voice' (1 Kings 19:12, Amplified). These promptings often come in the form of simple little instructions, like 'cast the net', 'speak to that person', 'contact X', 'invite Y to this event' etc. Obviously we need to test those promptings against the broader revelation of Scripture, and with the help of mature fellow Christians and leaders. We can also ask for and expect the Lord to bring confirming signs.

The great news is that when we've heard from the Lord and obeyed His instructions, we can see total transformation and turnaround. The disciples went from catching nothing to catching so much fish that they were unable to haul the net in. What a picture of abundance!

Whether it be in our daily lives, or in our ministries at church, such as our small groups, we can expect to see the huge abundance of God, as we welcome His intervention, and obey His instructions!

## Points to ponder

- Do you expect God to speak to you or have you given up even considering that that might be possible? Why do you think this is?
- Is it possible that you do not hear God, because something is blocking your hearing? Is there something that you need to remove?
- When was the last time you obeyed a 'prompting' of the Holy Spirit? What was the result?

## Prayer

*Thank You Jesus for loving me just as I am despite all my weaknesses. Today, Holy Spirit, I invite You to speak to me. May I be someone who listens to Your voice and quickly obeys. Anoint me to be a fisher of men; someone who draws people into Your kingdom. Amen.*

# Day 25

# FROM THE MIRACLE TO THE MIRACLE-MAKER

---

## John 21:7–14

Jesus' appearance to the disciples by the shore of Galilee starts with a miraculous catch of fish. But it doesn't end there. The point of the miracle is ultimately to point to the miracle-maker and involves an invitation to a closer walk with Him. Jesus did the miracle, in part, because it was His way of inviting the disciples and especially Peter into a renewed relationship with Himself.

Notice how the miracle leads to recognition of who Jesus is: 'Then the disciple whom Jesus loved said to Peter, "It is the Lord!"' (John 21:7). Significantly, the first to come to this realisation was 'the disciple whom Jesus loved', the one who had been closest to Him. So for us, too – as we develop an intimate daily walk we will be quick to recognise Him at work, calling us to a deeper relationship. If the contemplative disciple is the first to recognise Jesus, the activist Simon Peter is once again the first one to run to Him! 'As soon as Simon Peter heard him say, "It is the Lord," he wrapped his outer garment round him ... and jumped into the water. The other disciples followed in the boat, towing the net full of fish' (John 21:7–8). Wonderful, impulsive Peter! Notice here he doesn't let any sense of shame from the past hold him back, but he recognises in Jesus the inviting grace of God, and so runs to Him. This is a wonderful picture for us, too: no matter what we've done or not done we can and must run to Him, not from Him!

From recognition there comes the invitation to deeper relationship. Jesus is cooking and invites them to breakfast: 'Jesus said to them, "Bring some of the fish that you have just caught." So Simon Peter climbed back into the boat and dragged the net ashore. It was full of large fish, 153, but even with so many the net was not torn' (John 21:10–11). There has been lots of speculation about what the number 153 symbolises but the simplest explanation is that there were 153 fish! The point is that there were lots of fish, with the added miracle that the nets were not torn. When God blesses us, provides for us and fills our nets, there will be abundance and yet the nets won't break!

Then comes a second word of invitation: '"Come and have breakfast." None of the disciples dared ask him, "Who are you?" They knew it was the Lord. Jesus came, took the bread and gave it to them, and did the same with the fish' (John 21:12–13).

What a tender, practical, personal invitation. Here is the risen Jesus, who a short while ago had just triumphed over all the powers of sin and death, now concerned to give the tired and hungry disciples breakfast! On the one hand, this is a wonderful picture of Jesus, lovingly concerned for our physical and practical needs. On the other, since a meal was a sign of friendship and fellowship, it was also a way of providing a safe context to address the greater spiritual and emotional needs of one of the group, Simon Peter. Peter's restoration and recommissioning provide a fitting climax to this beautiful story, and will be the focus of the rest of the week.

So today, as you think about this wonderful passage, hear Jesus calling you to come and spend time with Him. He enjoys your company and He is ready and willing to refresh You by His presence. Know that He loves to come to you and meet with you anytime, anywhere. One of the dangers of being involved with a Christianity that focuses on a physical church is that we can have the peculiar view that God only speaks in this place. This paragraph is a good reminder that God can speak to us in the ordinary world.

I remember when I was a school teacher in Stamford, going out at lunch times to Burghley Park to walk and pray. Often I had a strong sense of Jesus coming to me and refreshing me in the midst of my day. A ministry colleague of mine also used to be a school teacher. He would try and get to school early and would pray over each chair before the day began. He commented to me that he could usually tell the difference between the days when he prayed in this way, and when he didn't.

Invite Jesus to come to you and expect Him to reveal Himself in the midst of your everyday activities.

## Points to ponder

- How quick are you to recognise the voice of God in your life?
- Do you believe that God enjoys your company?
- In what ways do you need His refreshing? (See Matt. 11: 28–29)

## Prayer

*Jesus, as I reflect on this passage, I am humbled and grateful that You want to spend time with me. Your company is refreshing and more satisfying than anyone or anything else this world can offer. Time with You is never wasted time! Today, I choose to rest in and be refreshed by You. Amen.*

# RESTORED BY JESUS

## John 21:15–17

Not only does Jesus help us in our present struggles, but He also comes to heal us from our past failures.

The incident in today's verses is especially significant because it is the first *recorded*[18] one-to-one conversation between Jesus and Peter since the denial. Jesus restores Peter in a very deliberate and dramatic way. First, He has just cooked the fish on a fire of burning coals. The word used is literally of a 'charcoal fire'. The only other place that this word is used in the entire New Testament was in John 18:18, when Peter was warming himself by the 'charcoal fire' when he denied Jesus. Secondly, Jesus deliberately addresses him as 'Simon, son of John' – not Peter, the 'rock' – highlighting his failure to live up to that name and to his need for restoration. Thirdly, Jesus is deliberately asking Peter the same basic question three times, since Peter had denied him three times, hence why Peter 'was hurt'.

What's happening here? Jesus is coming to Peter to heal him from his past failure. Jesus is deliberately reminding him of his denial, not to make him feel bad, but to bring him to a place of repentance, restoration and re-commissioning. Why does He have to face him up to the past? He wants Peter to own the problem. Jeremiah 17:9 informs us that 'the heart is deceitful above all things', or we could say that we have an innate ability for self-deception. In Alcoholics Anonymous, for example, one of the first keys to an alcoholic truly recovering is first acknowledging that he or she has actually got a problem. This is what Jesus is doing. He wants Peter to face up to who he is and what he has done so that he can be properly healed and restored, and not carry the problem with him into his future. The habit of God asking us to face our shortcomings with a question rather than directly accusing us is frequent in Scripture; it includes everything from 'where are you Adam?' to 'what are you doing Elijah?' and beyond. Even the best of us can suffer from self-deception.

Notice what Jesus doesn't do. He doesn't come and say, 'Now Peter, you remember how you denied me?' – of course Peter remembers. Instead Jesus goes to the root of the problem, 'Do you love more than these?' The 'more than these' could mean – more than fishing, could mean more than you love these men, or do you love me more than they do? There is no way of knowing for certain. What we can be sure of is that Jesus is highlighting that the heart of the matter is the matter of the heart: 'Peter, the reason you denied me was a love issue – you loved self, your reputation, what others thought of you – more than you loved me.' At the root of our greatest failures is our ultimate failure to fulfill the greatest commandment to 'Love the Lord your God with all your heart ... soul ... mind and ... strength' (Mark 12:30). Jesus knows that if Peter is not only going to know forgiveness, but is going to be fit for service, He has to come and deal with the heart issue! And He does!

Let me finish with this: In 1975, an angry man rushed through a Museum in Amsterdam until he reached Rembrandt's famous painting *Nightwatch*. Then he took out a knife and slashed it repeatedly before he could be stopped. Three years earlier, a distraught, hostile man slipped into St. Peter's Cathedral in Rome with a hammer and began to smash Michelangelo's beautiful sculpture *The Pieta*. Two cherished works of art were severely damaged. But what did officials do? Throw them out and forget about them? Absolutely not! Using the best experts, who worked with the utmost care and precision, they made every effort to restore the treasures.

You are far more precious to God than a priceless work of art. God made you, has a plan for you and sent Christ to restore you – from both self-inflicted damage and from hurts caused by others. The wonderful news is that when He restores, He makes all things new!

## Points to ponder

- Have you become aware today of any areas of your life where you have been living in self-deception rather than being honest with yourself, with others or with God?
- Do you need to repent of anything today?
- In what ways do you need restoration?

## Prayer

*Lord, You have searched my heart. You know all my thoughts, fears, flaws and habits. You know me inside out and yet You love me completely. I am all too aware of my shortcomings, yet I long to draw close to You. I bare my soul to You and bring all of my sin and brokenness to You, knowing that in Your presence I am safe. Come and restore me and make me new, so that I may love You fully. Amen.*

# RECOMMISSIONED BY JESUS

## John 21:15–17

The grace of God in this story is immense. Rather than be put off by Peter's denial and failure, Jesus comes not only to restore him but to recommission him. Throughout, He never stops believing in Peter and the call on his life. The great news for Peter and for every one of us is that the call is greater than the fall!

Thomas Edison was working on a first prototype light bulb and it took a whole team of men 24 straight hours to put just one together. The story goes that when Edison was finished with one light bulb, he gave it to a young boy helper, who nervously carried it up the stairs. Step by step he cautiously watched his hands, obviously frightened of dropping such a priceless piece of work. You've probably guessed what happened by now; the poor young fellow dropped the bulb at the top of the stairs. It took the entire team of men 24 more hours to make another bulb. Finally, tired and ready for a break, Edison was ready to have his bulb carried up the stairs. He gave it to the same young boy who dropped the first one. That's true forgiveness. He gave him a second chance!

I love the fact that our God gave Peter a second chance. Not only does He restore him, but He recommissions him. Read John 21:15–17 again. Notice the strong emphasis on lambs and sheep. The failed fisherman is called to be a great shepherd of God's people. Look at the results. A few weeks later, we see Peter standing up as the leader, preaching with boldness about the crucified, now risen and exalted Jesus, with the result that 3,000 are baptised and added to the church (Acts 2:14–41). Peter is then instrumental in the first recorded healing miracle of the Early Church (Acts 3). He preaches, is put in prison, is released by an angel, confronts sin with scary discernment and walks the streets of Jerusalem with such an anointing that the sick try just to get to his shadow so that they might be healed (Acts 4–5). And if that was not enough, he was given the privilege of being the first to preach the gospel to the Gentiles (Acts 10). Even today, 2,000 years on, he is honoured, along with the apostle Paul, as being the greatest and most significant founding leader of the Church universal.

What hope of restoration and recommissioning for us today! You may still be living in the pain and shame of past failure. You may never have accepted Christ, or have taken a wrong turn, drifted away from Him, and may be wondering whether God could or would ever forgive you, and whether you are capable of living a life that pleases Him. Take heart – look at how Jesus transformed Peter. Know that He is a loving Saviour who wants to come and help you face up to the past, forgive you, restore you, heal you and recommission you.

___

## Points to ponder

- Think about Peter. What inspires you most about his life?
- Think carefully about the things you believe God might be calling you to in life. In what ways are you investing in these things now? If you are not investing in your calling, perhaps you need to hear God recommissioning you today.

___

## Prayer

*Lord, I thank You for never giving up on me. I come to You today and repent for the times when, like Peter, I have not lived up to the calling that You have destined for me. I receive Your forgiveness and recommissioning. Thank You, Lord, for giving me a hope and a future. Amen!*

# BEWARE THE COMPARISON TRAP

—

## John 21:18–22

God has not only made each of us special and unique, but He has assigned to us our own unique destiny. One of the greatest enemies to us fulfilling that destiny is to fall into the comparison trap. We can either get into pride by comparing ourselves with others who we think are less blessed or gifted, or we can compare ourselves to others who we think have a better life or future, and get into jealousy and self-pity. Either way, we must escape the comparison trap if we want to fulfill the unique call of God on our lives.

Having just been gloriously restored and recommissioned, Peter starts to fall into the trap of comparing his future negatively with that of 'the disciple whom Jesus loved'. It comes on the back of Jesus' 'promise' of Peter being martyred: '"Very truly I tell you, when you were younger you dressed yourself and went where you wanted; but when you are old you will stretch out your hands, and someone else will dress you and lead you where you do not want to go." Jesus said this to indicate the kind of death by which Peter would glorify God. Then he said to him, "Follow me!"' (John 21:18–19). The reference to Peter's hands being stretched out alludes to martyrdom through crucifixion (and history would tell us that he was indeed faithful to the call of martyrdom).

I don't know how you would respond if you received this 'call'. I would probably have wanted to ask some further clarifying questions, such as: when, why, how painful, and is there any way to avoid it![19] But such is the folly and deception of human nature, that Peter immediately gets caught in the comparison trap, by being concerned about what would happen to the other disciple: 'Peter turned and saw that the disciple whom Jesus loved was following them. (This was the one who had leaned back against Jesus

at the supper and had said, "Lord, who is going to betray you?")
When Peter saw him, he asked, "Lord, what about him?" Jesus
answered, "If I want him to remain alive until I return, what is that
to you? You must follow me"' (John 21:20–22).

Here Jesus is giving Peter very helpful advice not to worry about
the call of God to another, but to concentrate on His own journey. The
good news is that Peter clearly learned from this rebuke. By the time
we see him in the book of Acts, he is exercising the unique leadership
role to which God had called him. It seems as if now, empowered by
the Holy Spirit, he is successfully following that unique path.

Like Peter, you have a unique calling from God. He has specifically
gifted you to help you fulfill that calling. So, rather than letting
comparisons with others derail you, learn to rejoice in who God has
made you to be, and what He has called you to do. But that is only
part of the picture. In the church, no one person has all the gifts or
is called to be a one man/one woman superstar! Rather, God has
deliberately placed us in a 'body' and we are called to rejoice in other
people's gifts and callings, knowing that it is when we work together
and honour one another that God is most glorified and the work is
most fruitful. So, thank God for those differently gifted people God
has placed around you. Celebrate with them, and thank God for the
gifts, talents and calling that He has given them. Together you will
see great things accomplished, to the glory of His name!

## Points to ponder

- Do you tend to compare yourself to anybody else? If so,
  what do you think is the root cause of that?
- Why is it so tempting to concentrate on other people and
  how they are doing? On a scale of one to ten, how readily do
  you rejoice in the successes of those close to you? Is there
  anybody you find it particularly difficult to rejoice with in
  success and if so, why?
- Thank God for your own uniqueness and ask Him to help you
  become increasingly aware of the gifts and strengths He
  has placed within you.

## Prayer

*Lord, 'I praise You because I am fearfully and wonderfully made; Your works are wonderful, I know that full well' (Psa. 139:14). I thank You for seeing and knowing every detail of my life. Not one thing is hidden from You. I come to You today and apologise for the times when I have compared myself to others. I recognise that in doing so, I insult You and Your craftsmanship. You are good all the time and You know exactly what You are doing! I surrender my life to You afresh today. Lead me forward into my unique destiny. Help me to celebrate the gifts of others and work them for Your glory! Amen!*

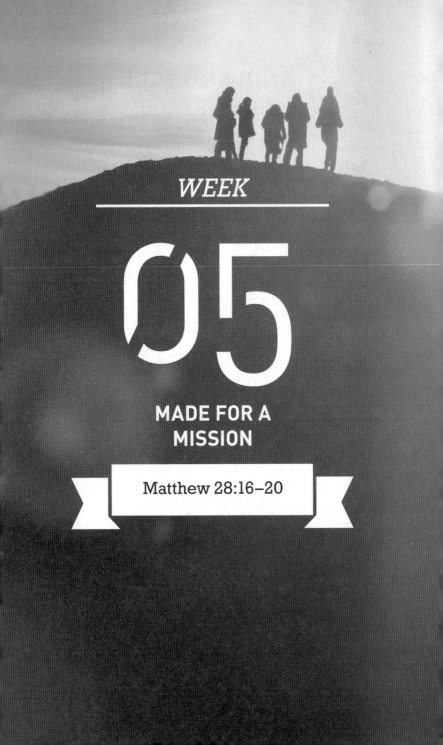

*WEEK*

# 05

## MADE FOR A
## MISSION

Matthew 28:16–20

# KNOWING YOUR LIFE PURPOSE

—

## Matthew 28:16–20

You are not an accident. You were born for a purpose. God designed you that you might come to know Him, be loved by Him, and fulfill *His* purpose for your life. In the words of Rick Warren in his bestselling book, *The Purpose Driven Life*: 'If you want to know why you were placed on this planet, you must begin with God. You were born *by* his purpose and *for* his purpose.'[20]

During the 40 days between His resurrection and return to heaven, Jesus taught, and repeatedly emphasised, that He was giving His followers the greatest possible assignment: the continuation of His mission on earth. This week we are going to be looking at a meeting where this purpose was most comprehensively explained. It took place on a mountain in Galilee and has become known as the great commission: 'Then Jesus came to them and said, "All authority in heaven and on earth has been given to me. Therefore go and make disciples of all nations, baptising them in the name of the Father and of the Son and of the Holy Spirit, and teaching them to obey everything I have commanded you. And surely I am with you always, to the very end of the age' (Matt. 28:18-20).

The great commission is a useful phrase, especially if we remember that a commission can be seen as a co-mission; something we do with someone. Jesus wants us to work *with* Him.

Exactly how we fulfill Jesus' calling to us will vary from person to person, depending on our background, gifting, personality and geography. Nevertheless, each of us has the same fundamental calling to love God and to love others as ourselves (the great commandment – more on Day 34) and to go, preach the gospel and make disciples of all nations (the great commission). Hence, we can neatly summarise our life purpose as 'a great commitment to the great commandment and the great commission'.

The great commission is all about people being called and sent by Jesus and it is fascinating to see that almost every encounter with Jesus in the 40 days involves some kind of commissioning:

- Mary is 'commissioned' to tell the male disciples on the first Easter morning and does so (John 20:17–18)
- The women at the tomb are told: 'Go and tell my brothers to go to Galilee; there they will see me' (Matt. 28:10)
- Even though they are not (as far as we know) given a specific commissioning order, the two who meet Jesus at Emmaus immediately go back to Jerusalem to tell 'the Eleven and those with them' (Luke 24:33)
- John's Gospel records a specific commissioning on the first Easter Sunday evening: 'As the Father has sent me, I am sending you' (John 20:21)
- Peter receives a three-fold commissioning after breakfast by the Sea of Galilee: 'Feed my lambs ... Take care of my sheep ... Feed my sheep' (John 21:15–19)
- The disciples are commissioned on a mountain in Galilee (Matt. 28:16–20 – the focus of this week's study)
- At the end of Mark's Gospel there is what is called 'the longer ending' (Mark 16:15–20). Although there is considerable debate as to whether it was an original part of Mark's Gospel it is very early and records something that parallels the great commission of Matthew
- The disciples are commissioned during Jesus' final days in Jerusalem (Luke 24:45–49; Acts 1:3–8 – the focus of next week's study).

This repeated pattern of calling and sending by Jesus suggests that this was extraordinarily important to Him. It is a reminder to us that the authentic Christian faith is not about passively receiving forgiveness and other blessings from God, but rather actively obeying Christ. Our faith is supposed to overflow in fulfilling God's saving purposes for others and our world.

It is worth emphasising that the heart of our mission is the call to 'make disciples'. Put simply it is a call for followers of Jesus, to go and make other followers of Jesus – not simply to convert people in the sense of adding numbers to the Christian fellowship – but to see their lives transformed in and through a relationship with Jesus Christ.

## Points to ponder

- How aware are you that God has a life purpose for you?
- In what ways have you experienced Jesus transforming your life? How might you change aspects of your life to become more involved in transforming the lives of other people?
- Do you have a sense of what God is calling you to do? Are you asking Him to show you?

## Prayer

*Lord Jesus, I thank You that You have not only come to save me, but You have given me a divine purpose for my life. I ask You to send Your Spirit of wisdom and revelation to help me know You better and to know the calling on my life (Eph. 1:17–18). I open my heart to You and invite You to speak to me, and give me the boldness to fulfill Your will for my life. Amen.*

# TRANSFORMED TO TRANSFORM OTHERS

## Matthew 28:16–17

Yesterday we highlighted the importance of each of us fulfilling our life purpose – to love God, love people and to make other followers of Jesus. However, before we can effectively fulfill this call to go and see others' lives transformed, it is vital that we allow God to transform our lives first.

As we look at the early disciples we can be encouraged by the fact that their transformation was a process and was definitely not instantaneous. In spite of spending over three years with Jesus before He was crucified and many days having seen Him alive again, some of Jesus' followers still struggled to fully believe. You can hardly blame them. Death is naturally the most final of things, to which there is normally no sequel! Significantly, just prior to Jesus giving the great commission we read: 'Then the eleven disciples went to Galilee, to the mountain where Jesus had told them to go. When they saw him, they worshipped him; but some doubted' (Matt. 28:16–17). Notice here the two responses: worship and doubt.

First, let's look at the priority of worship. The word here literally means to prostrate, or fall down in attitude of humility before a greater person. It is a bodily expression of a reverent attitude of mind. At the sight of the risen Jesus the disciples prostrate themselves before Jesus, the risen Lord and Messiah.

Secondly, we have the surprising admission that some still doubted. Given that we are already some time into the 40 days, and Jesus has appeared to His disciples on several occasions already, what are we to make of this? Commentators have puzzled as to whether the 'some' who doubted were a different group to the eleven disciples, or whether they included some or all of the Eleven. Part of the explanation concerns the specific meaning of the translated word 'doubt', which here doesn't so much mean 'unbelief', but rather 'hesitancy'. So we could more helpfully say that there was both worship and hesitancy going on in the same meeting![21]

Although we cannot be sure whether these 'hesitant' ones included the Eleven, we can be fairly certain that they were disciples of Jesus. They must have been in order to have obeyed Jesus' instruction to go to Galilee, and to gather on a mountain in expectation of meeting Him. In spite of this and the fact that the risen Christ does appear and is worshipped, they are still hesitant towards Him. This may have been due to the fact that they were Jews, whose fiercely held core belief was that there was only one God, and no one else could come beside Him, as Jesus has. Or it may simply have been the fact that some were *still on a journey*. In the words of one commentator: 'they still were hesitant; and their failure to understand his repeated predictions of his resurrection, compounded with their despair after his crucifixion, worked to maintain their hesitancy for some time before they came to full faith. *Jesus' resurrection did not instantly transform men of little faith and faltering understanding into spiritual giants*' (my emphasis).[22]

How should we respond to this mixed reaction to the risen Christ? First, by acknowledging that the best and most appropriate way to acknowledge His Lordship is to bow down and worship Him, giving our whole lives to Him (see Rom. 12:1). Before we become great witnesses, we must learn to become great worshippers! Secondly, we can be reassured that if we still sometimes feel of 'little faith and faltering understanding' we are in good company! Our hesitancy doesn't disqualify us for the mission. Yet at the same time, it is worth noticing that this event occurs before the giving of the Holy Spirit, one of whose tasks is to convince people of who Jesus is. Today we must invite the Holy Spirit to reveal Jesus to us in a new and greater way, so that we can leave our hesitancy behind and wholeheartedly follow Him.

## Points to ponder

- How can you worship the risen Christ with the use of your time, money, gifts and relationships? How regular and enthusiastic are you in acts of personal and public worship?
- In what ways do you need to bow or kneel before Jesus? Ask Him to show you any areas of your life where you may be holding back from Him, in hesitancy.

## Prayer

*Lord, I want to thank You for Your grace and patience towards me. I acknowledge that I am still on a journey. I want to grow in a greater revelation of how wonderful You are. I choose to lay aside my hesitancy and offer You my whole life in worshipful surrender. Amen.*

# THE SOURCE OF OUR MISSION

## Matthew 28:18

At the start of this week we focused on the importance of finding and fulfilling God's purpose for our lives. Today we will emphasise just how important it is that we turn to *Him* for this discovery. Put simply, if we look out to the world or search within ourselves to find our purpose, we will end up confused or off track. But if we look to God and to His Son, Jesus Christ, things will become clear. Significantly, therefore, before Jesus commissioned His disciples, He focused on His authority to do so, in this stunning declaration: 'All authority in heaven and on earth has been given to me' (Matt. 28:18).

First, it is worth noting that Jesus' authority was 'given' to Him – evidently from His Father, God the Creator of the heavens and the earth. In the light of the clearly Trinitarian statement in the verse that follows it ('in the name of the Father and of the Son and of the Holy Spirit'), we can begin to grasp the full implications of this authority. Jesus, the man who was anointed, crucified and is now risen, is also the divine Son of God, and has received His authority both *as* the Son of God and *from* God the Father.

Second, notice the extent of this authority, which is universal – 'in heaven and on earth'. Previously, in Matthew's Gospel, Jesus has made claim to having 'authority on earth to forgive sins' (Matt. 9:6).[23] More strikingly still, He declares that 'All things have been committed to me by my Father' (Matt. 11:27). Now, after His atoning death and triumphant resurrection His authority over all things has been gloriously confirmed, and is now extended to include heaven as well as earth. (See also Eph. 1:20–23; Col. 1:16–20; Heb. 1:1–3.)

The implications of this claim are huge. In the context of the great commission that immediately follows, it highlights that

Christ alone has true authority over all of creation. This is an assurance to His disciples, then and now, that when we go to share the good news we are not going in our authority but in the authority of the King of kings and Lord of lords! He alone understands the future of the world and what's best for all of humanity. Yet Jesus is not only Lord of the world and its future, He is also rightfully Lord of our lives – He uniquely understands us and knows how we can play our part in changing the lives of other people. He is sovereign over all!

Until I became a Christian, I had no real understanding of my life purpose, other than a vague desire to be 'happy'. Yet as soon as I invited Christ into my life, I had a deep and abiding sense that I was made on purpose and for a purpose. I quickly realised that this purpose involved being loved by, and in return loving, the God who had made me and saved me, and that this love was to overflow in making a difference in other people's lives.

The way that God revealed His purpose for my life is the same way that He wants to reveal His assignment to you: through His Word (the Bible), and by His Holy Spirit. Over the next few days, we will be looking in more detail at God's call as revealed in the Bible, especially contained in the great commission. But we will also be positioning ourselves to hear more specific and personal directions for our lives that come through the revelation of His Holy Spirit.

I remember as a young Christian listening to the story of the pastor of what was then the largest church in history. When asked how he had been able to accomplish so much, he simply replied: 'I pray and I obey!' Those words literally changed my life. I quickly realised that prayer was not a monologue but a dialogue, and that a priority in prayer was listening to the Master and heeding His directions. Since that time, I have sought to prioritise a listening relationship with the Lord. Many times He has spoken to me clearly concerning His will for my life. The great assurance that I have is that Jesus really is the Lord of heaven and earth, and that when He speaks I know that He has the best plans and purposes for my life, and for those He has called me to reach out to. My part is to trust and obey!

## Points to ponder

- How do you respond to the thought that God alone has the ultimate plan for your life and that you were born by His purpose and for His purpose?
- Think about what you want to do for God and think about what obstacles discourage you. Remind yourself that Christ is bigger than any of them.
- Do you need to consciously surrender to Christ and His will for your life, today?
- Invite the Holy Spirit to speak to you today, both as you have set aside time with Him and as you go about your daily business.

## Prayer

*Lord, I acknowledge that You alone know what's best for me. I ask You to forgive me for the times when I looked elsewhere for the source of my purpose. Please speak to me today and for the rest of these 40 days. I want to know Your will for me and fulfill the plans You have for me. Amen.*

# THE CALL TO GO ON A MISSION

## Matthew 28:19

At the heart of the great commission is the call to 'Go'. Having made a statement concerning His authority, Jesus then commissions His disciples: 'Therefore *go* and make disciples of all nations' (Matt. 28:19, my emphasis). This focus on making disciples *of all nations* highlights the universality of the gospel: God's call to the Jewish people to come to Him is now broadened out into a call, through the disciples, to all the nations of the world. This of course includes a mandate for overseas missions, but more broadly it is a commission to take the gospel to everyone everywhere! For most of us this will mean taking the good news to those around us whether it be our family, friends, neighbours, work colleagues. The question is how? Put simply, through our works, our words and with wonders.

First, we must go and share the good news through our good works.

Earlier in his Gospel, Matthew records the famous Sermon on the Mount. One of the remarkable statements Jesus makes to His disciples is this: 'You are the light of the world. A town built on a hill cannot be hidden. Neither do people light a lamp and put it under a bowl. Instead they put it on a stand, and it gives light to everyone in the house. In the same way, let your light shine before others, that they may see your good deeds and glorify your Father in heaven' (Matt. 5:14–16).

The point is clear. Since we *are* light, we must let our light shine by the way we live our lives. Then others will see our good deeds and praise the God we love and serve. Very often others will be first attracted to the gospel by our actions before they will receive our words. Whether this be with a consistent lifestyle of integrity, authenticity and joy, or acts of kindness, these good works are an essential part of fulfilling the great commission and of going and 'preaching the gospel without words'. But we must not stop there!

Second, we must share the good news through speaking words of life.

This comes out more clearly in the ancient version of the great commission found at the end of Mark's Gospel: 'He said to them, "Go into all the world and *preach the gospel* to all creation. Whoever believes and is baptised will be saved' (Mark 16:15–16, my emphasis). This is hugely important and highlights that central to our mission is the call to preach or proclaim the good news, an emphasis that has come through strongly during the 40 days. We have good news, in fact the best news ever, so we must not keep it to ourselves, but go and tell others. Why? Because it is only through the hearing of the good news that people can believe and be saved (Rom. 10:14–17). Yet this is something that many Christians find really difficult, even intimidating. Sometimes this is due to a fear of being inadequate, or of losing reputation or of being rejected. What is liberating is to realise that God wants to use each one of us and work with our own personality and style, whether we are naturally loud or quiet, extrovert or introvert.

I sometimes find it helpful to think of sharing my faith under the theme of telling stories. Particularly if I am engaging with people I don't know very well, I find it is usually important to listen to them first and hear *their* story. Sometimes, and without forcing the conversation, it is appropriate then to tell *my* story, which may include something about my faith, my conversion, or the way Christ has changed and is changing my life. This then can lead on to an opportunity to tell *His* story – of how God created us, how we rejected Him, how Christ came to rescue us, and how we can respond to Him and be saved. It may be that you don't yet feel ready to do this, but what you can do is invite the person to come and hear someone else preach the good news – at a church guest event or something like an Alpha course.

So, we are called to go and *show* the good news through our works, and *tell* the good news through our words. But there is a third dimension that was strongly present in the Early Church, and is very evident in many parts of the world today: God will confirm His Word with signs and wonders.

This is implicit in the closing words of Matthew's Gospel: 'And surely I am with you always, to the very end of the age' (Matt. 28:20), and is made more explicit in the closing words of Mark's account: 'Then the disciples went out and preached everywhere, and the Lord worked with them and confirmed his word by the signs that accompanied it' (Mark 16:20). From a few verses earlier it seems evident that these 'signs' include healing the sick and casting out demons. Moreover, these signs were not to be restricted to the ministry of the apostles but were to include all 'those who believe: in my name' (Mark 16:17). This supernatural dimension, often missing in western churches, is nevertheless something that we can expect as we go and share the good news.

So, let's go out with words, works and wonders and let others hear and see the good news of God's transforming grace through Jesus!

___

## Points to ponder

- Who are the people in your world to whom you are seeking to reach out? Could you start praying for their salvation daily?
- Is there someone in your world whom you could bless today? It doesn't have to be something extravagant – it might be a kind word or a small gift – just something that shows appreciation of them.

___

## Prayer

*Lord I ask You to fill me anew with Your love for those who don't know You. Please give me an increased sensitivity to the promptings of Your Spirit and the boldness to share the good news in the things I say and do. Jesus, may my life so reflect You, that others may be drawn to You. Amen!*

# Day

# 33 BAPTISM

## Matthew 28:19

Over a number of years of pastoral ministry I have had the joy of seeing many people baptised. This dramatic acting out of the transforming work of Christ in the life of a believer is not only a defining moment for the individuals involved, but is a great witness to those around, as well as a tremendous cause for rejoicing for the local church.

So what is baptism and why is it so important? The word 'baptism' comes from the Greek *baptizo* and simply means to immerse or dip. From the outset, the Gospel writers give baptism a central place in the Jesus story. John the 'Baptist' sets the agenda with his baptism for repentance, and Jesus Himself chooses to be baptised by John in the Jordan River – not because He needed to repent of sin, but because He wanted to set a pattern for His followers (Matt. 3). Jesus further highlights the importance of baptism by making it an integral part of the great commission. In fact, immediately after the command to go and make disciples is the follow-up call to go 'baptising them in the name of the Father and of the Son and of the Holy Spirit' (Matt. 28:19).

Significantly, baptism follows rather than precedes the call to 'make disciples'. In other words baptism doesn't make a person a Christian; it is a sign that someone has become one. Moreover, the Bible teaches us that there are certain pre-conditions before someone is baptised into the Christian faith. In Acts 2 at the end of Peter's Pentecost sermon, the people asked, 'what shall we do?' to which Peter replied, 'Repent and be baptised, every one of you, in the name of Jesus Christ' (Acts 2:37–38). Notice that repentance precedes baptism. First, you repent (literally 'change your mind'), and then you are baptised.

If repentance is a pre-condition for baptism, then so, too, is faith. In Mark's version of the great commission, Jesus again gives baptism a central place, but this time the emphasis is on first believing and then being baptised: 'Whoever believes and is baptised will be saved, but whoever does not believe will be condemned' (Mark 16:16). Notice that baptism is pictured as an essential part of salvation ('will be saved'), yet not being baptised will not lead to condemnation. After all, in Luke 23:32–43, we see that the thief on the cross was not baptised, but Jesus promised that He would be in heaven. Only unbelief will keep a person out of God's favour.

So what does baptism signify? In Romans 6 Paul uses the language of baptism to describe what it means to be a Christian: 'don't you know that all of us who were baptised into Christ Jesus were baptised into his death? We were therefore buried with him through baptism into death in order that, just as Christ was raised from the dead through the glory of the Father, we too may live a new life' (Rom. 6:3–4). Although baptism is not the means by which we enter into a relationship with Christ, in New Testament times it so closely followed conversion that Paul uses the picture of outward baptism to depict our inward union with Christ. Powerful language indeed!

A further picture is found in 1 Corinthians 10:2, where Paul refers back to the Old Testament people of God as being 'baptised into Moses in the cloud and in the sea'. The 'sea' is the Red Sea and is a reminder of how the children of Israel were finally rescued from the slavery of Egypt, which in turn opened the way for them to enter into their long promised inheritance in the land of Canaan. In the same way, it is possible to see this applied to Christian baptism. Once a person becomes a Christian, God does a wonderful internal work of making them new and making them His child. When a person is baptised, it is a public expression of this reality and is a way of saying: 'I am leaving my past life behind with all that might hold me back, and I am stepping into all that God has for me.'

I remember how, shortly after becoming a Christian and reading this account of Jesus being baptised, I had a clear sense that if I was to be a fully devoted follower of Christ, I needed to follow His example and be baptised, too. So, in obedience to Jesus' example and teaching, I was baptised. Quite unexpectedly and dramatically as I came up from the water, I had a profound sense of God's presence, and a clear awareness that this step had closed a door to my past, and opened up a new door to God's great future for me.

If baptism is so central to the great commission, it is important that we give it an appropriate place in our local churches and in the lives of individuals. For those of us who are already baptised disciples, we must help new converts understand the importance of publicly declaring their faith through baptism. If you are a follower of Christ, but have not been baptised, can I encourage you to do so as soon as possible!

---

## Points to ponder

- Have you been baptised? If not, ask the Lord and talk to local church leaders about the next steps for you.
- For those who have been baptised, what do you remember about it and what significance does it have for you today?
- Have you recently seen other people at your church being baptised? If so, take a few moments to pray for them to keep growing in their walk with God.

---

## Prayer

*Lord, I celebrate that in Christ I am now dead to sin and alive to You (Rom. 6:11). Thank You for washing me, sanctifying me and justifying me in Christ (1 Cor. 6:11) and for raising me up with Him and seating me in heavenly places (Eph. 2:6). I make a choice to live in the fullness of all that You have won for me. May my public declaration of faith be an overflow of my inward devotion to You. In Jesus' name. Amen.*

# TEACHING
# OBEDIENCE

## Matthew 28:20

The New Testament makes it absolutely clear that we are saved by grace through faith, and not by our works (eg Eph. 2:8–9). What then are we to make of the centrality of Jesus' emphasis on obedience in the great commission, expressed in these words: 'teaching them to obey everything I have commanded' (Matt. 28:20)?

I find it helps to consider this question by looking at the difference between legalism, licence and liberty. We could summarise the Christian life as a call to liberty or freedom – which keeps us from the opposite extremes of what we might call legalism and licence. It's as if we are called to drive up a highway of freedom, avoiding the ditches of legalism and licence on either side.

Let's take legalism first. This in essence is a system of religion that is based on law-keeping as the way to please God. The problem is that none of us can keep all the commandments of God. Therefore Christ came to keep and fulfil the law perfectly and then to die in our place to forgive us for our law-breaking and give us His righteousness! (Rom. 3:22–24; 8:1–4; Gal. 3:15–17).

Let's take licence next. Sadly, some Christians who rejoice in their freedom from the Law misunderstand and misappropriate their freedom as a licence to please themselves, rather than being set free from the Law and sin in order to live a life that pleases God (Gal. 5:13).

If we can avoid the ditches of legalism and licence we can live lives of great liberty! True liberty comes from being inwardly transformed by the grace of Christ, and by being regularly filled with the Spirit, enabling us to live in such a way that honours God and liberates us (Gal. 5:16–18). This life includes a new freedom to obey the commands of God, as re-interpreted through the life and ministry of Jesus.

With this as a backdrop, what are the commands that Jesus is referring to here in the great commission? Part of the answer lies in looking back to the wonderful principles contained in the Sermon on the Mount (Matt. 5–7). Here, as well as the Beatitudes and the reminder of the importance of giving, fasting, praying, and loving God more than money, we have Jesus teaching concerning the 'moral law'. Some people wrongly teach that since we are free from law-keeping and the sacrificial system of the Old Testament as a way to being accepted by God, that the moral law, as summarised in the Ten Commandments, no longer has any relevance to us today. The teachings of Jesus make abundantly clear that this is simply not the case. Rather than rejecting the commandments, Jesus re-interprets them and even lifts the bar by talking about heart attitudes in addition to outward actions. So instead of just re-emphasising the importance of, for example, not committing murder or adultery, He highlights that we must stay away from the deeper heart issues of anger and lust (see Matt. 5:17–48).

Perhaps the most telling summary of Jesus' interpretation of the commandments comes in answer to a question from a religious expert who asked Him: 'which is the greatest commandment in the Law?' (Matt. 22:36). Jesus' reply is a masterful bringing together of the whole moral law under two headings: '"Love the Lord your God with all your heart and with all your soul and with all your mind." This is the first and greatest commandment. And the second is like it: "Love your neighbour as yourself." All the Law and the Prophets hang on these two commandments' (Matt. 22:37–40). Put simply, if we want to obey everything that Jesus has commanded us, then we are to love God and to love people! If we add to this Jesus' new commandment in John: 'love one another. As I have loved you, so you must love one another' (John 13:34), we come to the heart of what Christian obedience looks like.

Of course, this doesn't mean that we are to go back to law-keeping as a way to get accepted before God. Rather, having been made right with God and having been filled with the Spirit, we can live lives of loving Him and others in a way that truly glorifies Him and fulfills us.

## Points to ponder

- Are you truly living in your grace-given freedom or do you tend to fall into the ditches of legalism or licence? Which one do you fall for most?
- Why not take some time today to ask the Holy Spirit to help you to walk free from these things.

## Prayer

*Father, I want to thank You that through Jesus, I can be freed from legalism and license and live a life of liberty. Please fill me with Your Holy Spirit so that I can obey the commands of Jesus. Help me to love You wholeheartedly, and to love others in the way that You've loved me. In a world full of difficult and complex decisions help me listen to the guidance from Your Spirit. Amen.*

# THE PROMISE OF HIS PRESENCE

## Matthew 28:20

In spite of social networking and modern communications many people today still feel lonely. Yet one of the greatest blessings of Christianity and one of the greatest lessons of the 40 days is that because Jesus is alive and is now present in the world by His Spirit, we need never feel alone! This theme comes out clearly through Matthew's Gospel. In the first chapter Jesus is revealed as 'Immanuel', 'God with us' (Matt. 1:23), and in the very last verse of the last chapter, we have this promise of Christ's abiding presence: 'And surely I am with you always, to the very end of the age' (Matt. 28:20). The *certainty* of this promise is emphasised in the word 'surely'; the *extent* of the promise is highlighted in the use of the word 'always' (which literally means 'all the days'), and the *duration* of the promise is stressed in the phrase 'to the end of the age.' A wonderful promise indeed!

This promise was fulfilled through the ascension of Jesus at the end of the 40 days (more on Day 40), and through the outpouring of the Spirit on the Day of Pentecost. As those who are living post-Pentecost, it means that, amazingly, we are now living in a better 'age' than the disciples were when Jesus was physically present with them. This truth is highlighted in Jesus' words recorded in John's Gospel: 'But very truly I tell you, it is for your good that I am going away. Unless I go away, the Advocate will not come to you; but if I go, I will send him to you' (John 16:7). Many Christians today fail to grasp the blessings of what we enjoy with Jesus in heaven and the Spirit on earth. They say that if only they could have been here when Jesus was on earth, and witnessed first-hand His miracles, and audibly heard His teaching, *then* they could believe and receive transformation. Or you yourself may be in the position of having journeyed through these 40 Days, and studied the post-resurrection appearances, and found yourself wishing that you could have been there in person with the early disciples and seen Jesus with your own eyes.

While there's no doubt that to have experienced Jesus' physical presence would have been great, there were two main reasons why He couldn't stay on the earth, and why it's better that He is now in heaven and the Holy Spirit is here on the earth. First, during His time on earth Jesus was limited in His presence. Even in His resurrected state – and able to suddenly appear – He could only be in one place at one time. He could not be at the Garden of Gethsemane, the Road to Emmaus, a room in Jerusalem, beside the Sea of Galilee or on a mountain all at the same time. Therefore, He had to appear to them, one person or group at a time. And He certainly couldn't be in Israel and England, India or America simultaneously! Secondly, while He was on the earth, He alone had the power of the Spirit. During His earthly ministry and the 40 days after the resurrection, He was the only one with the knowledge and the power to change lives. On a few occasions, He gave His disciples a temporary power and authority (Matt. 10:1) – but they did not possess the abiding, indwelling, empowering presence of the Spirit that was needed to spread the good news.

The ascension of Jesus and the outpouring of the Spirit solved both problems, because Jesus could now come to His disciples as the omnipresent Christ, in and through the person of the Holy Spirit. As we read again in John's Gospel, Jesus makes this remarkable promise: 'And I will ask the Father, and he will give you another advocate to help you and be with you for ever ... I will not leave you orphans; I will come to you' (John 14:16,18). Here's the staggering truth: we are never alone. Through the unlimited Spirit of God who comes not just to be *with* us but to live *in* us, Jesus is personally present all of the time! The same Jesus who taught, healed and delivered, who was crucified and is now risen, is now with us 24/7 for the rest of our lives. He is here to strengthen and comfort us in our own walk with Him, as well as empower us as we seek to carry out His great commission.

## Points to ponder

- What could you do, practically, to remind yourself on a regular basis of the abiding presence of God with you? (Some people have put an hourly reminder on their phone.)
- Are there any situations you are currently facing where you feel utterly inadequate? Invite God into those situations and ask Him to give you a greater awareness of His presence with you. When faced with temptation, why not think about the presence of Christ with you?

## Prayer

*Lord Jesus, I thank You for the amazing truth that You are with me always. Help me to welcome and recognise Your presence in my daily life. In times of joy, times of sorrow and times of temptation, I know Holy Spirit that You are ready and willing to give me guidance, peace and wisdom. Fill me now again and empower me to fulfill Your great commission. Amen.*

# 06

## FINAL
## PREPARATIONS

Acts 1:1–11; Luke 24:45–53

# IMPORTANCE
# OF PREPARATION

## Acts 1:1–3

In any sphere of life we usually have to undergo a period of preparation before enjoying any position of real responsibility and influence. In the Old Testament, Joseph underwent 13 years of tough training before suddenly being called to be 'Prime Minister' of Egypt. Moses endured 40 years in the desert before he was ready to be Israel's deliverer. Jesus' disciples were fast-tracked in three and a half years; the 40 days being the final stages in their preparation to become world changers.

This emphasis on preparation comes out clearly in the first few verses of Acts, where Luke writes: 'In my former book [the Gospel of Luke], Theophilus, I wrote about all that Jesus began to do and to teach until the day he was taken up to heaven, after giving instructions through the Holy Spirit to the apostles he had chosen. After his suffering, he presented himself to them and gave many convincing proofs that he was alive. He appeared to them over a period of forty days and spoke about the kingdom of God' (Acts 1:1–3).

This summary clearly highlights that the main reason why Jesus stayed on earth for 40 days after His resurrection, rather than ascending to heaven immediately, was to complete the 'training programme' for the disciples.

As I look back on my own life and at the history of KingsGate church, I am grateful (in hindsight!) for our own early season of preparation. For Karen and me the first four years in Peterborough were particularly tough. We were young, still working on issues in our marriage and learning to parent our six-month-old daughter, Emily. I was starting a new job in teaching, while finishing a university thesis in holidays and my 'spare time'. In addition, we knew hardly anyone in this totally new city and virtually nothing about church leadership. Then there were the financial pressures. We moved at the height of the property boom in 1988, managed to buy almost the cheapest house on the market (with damp in the walls and rotting windows), and yet still needed a mortgage that left us regularly praying for extra money to cover basic bills, and with virtually no disposable income. We held our first ever church meeting with nine people in this new home on the day that we moved in, with the peeling wallpaper providing an interesting backdrop. After a gruelling 18 months the church had grown to 15 before experiencing a 'back-door revival', and went down to six! I was ready to hand my resignation in to the Lord but He wouldn't accept!

Yet throughout this season the Lord was teaching us to put roots deep down in Him, at a time when little was showing above ground. We grew closer together as a family, had our second daughter, Annabel, started seeing a small core of people added and experienced miracles of financial provision on a regular basis, often at the eleventh hour. A few years later, I was being prayed for by an older man of God, who while praying pronounced over me: 'The greater the call, the more radical the surgery!' It wasn't exactly the word I was looking for but I came to realise that the preparation season, while often tough, had been necessary for what lay ahead.

Seasons of preparation don't necessarily just happen at the beginning of life and ministry, but can come later in life at a 'half-time' moment or before a new season of breakthrough. In one sense God's preparation of us through the Holy Spirit to make us more gloriously Christ-like is a work that is ongoing in every season of life (2 Cor. 3:17–18). Yet there are also specific times when it seems as if this is the primary emphasis, when the season is more about God helping us do root work rather than fruit work! It may be one of those seasons in your life right now. If so, can I encourage you to co-operate with the Holy Spirit and invite Him to do the necessary work in you, so that He can do all that He wants to do *through* you. May you take encouragement from the writer of the Hebrews: 'At the time, discipline isn't much fun. It always feels like it's going against the grain. Later, of course, it pays off handsomely, for it's the well-trained who find themselves mature in their relationship with God' (Heb. 12:11, *The Message*).

## Points to ponder

- In one sense, God is always at work in us, preparing us for what lies ahead. In what ways do you feel God is at work in you right now? How are you co-operating with the work of the Spirit?
- God seems to rarely allow leaders to appear without them having to go through a long period of training. What advantages do you think there are in leaders being trained for a long time before they are allowed to lead God's people?
- If you feel you have been in preparation for a long time, take some time to read about how God worked in the life of Joseph. His story in found in Genesis 37–50.

## Prayer

*Lord, I thank You that You love me and want the best for me. I make a choice today to embrace Your preparation, knowing that You have good plans for my life. Help me to learn the easier way by listening to Your voice and responding to Your promptings. Help me to grow in faith and patience so that I inherit the fullness of Your promises (Heb. 6:12). Amen.*

# CONVINCING PROOFS

---

## Acts 1:3

Central to Jesus' preparation of His disciples during the 40 days was giving them first-hand evidence that He was alive from the dead. Unsurprisingly, this is highlighted in Luke's summary: 'After his suffering, he presented himself to them and gave many convincing proofs that he was alive. He appeared to them over a period of forty days and spoke about the kingdom of God' (Acts 1:3). If the providing of 'convincing proofs' was important then, it is still important today. After all, the resurrection is something that marks Jesus out as being different to every other religious leader in history. If Jesus was not raised from the dead then He is nothing but a tragic curiosity of ancient Jewish history. But if He was raised from the dead then He is truly worth following.

So, as we come towards the end of our study let's step back and summarise the New Testament evidence for the resurrection:

**Jesus' absence from the tomb.** All four gospel writers testify that on the first Easter morning, Jesus' body was no longer in the tomb. The fullest account is contained in John chapter 20 (see Week 1). Mary Magdalene's visit to the tomb and the subsequent visit by Peter and the disciple Jesus loved, contained a number of 'convincing proofs' concerning the absence of Jesus:

- The stone, possibly weighing as much one to two tonnes, had been rolled away from the entrance to the tomb.
- Women, whose value as witnesses was considered to be distinctly second-rate, were the first people to claim the tomb was empty.
- Neither Mary nor the male disciples were expecting the resurrection - nor was anyone else for that matter!
- The grave clothes were still there, and had collapsed as if the body of Jesus had simply passed through.
- The head piece was set aside in an orderly fashion.

All of this has a convincing ring of authenticity and emphasises that Jesus' body was clearly no longer in the tomb. So, what had happened to His body? Some have suggested that the disciples had stolen the body but this seems highly implausible. It raises huge questions such as how would they have overcome the guard, and if they had stolen it, why would they live the rest of their lives, and risk their lives, for the sake of a dead Messiah? (Church tradition tells us that only one disciple, John, died in his bed. The rest were martyred.) The suggestion that the authorities stole the body seems similarly suspect: they had nothing to gain by this, and in fact, much to lose. If they had done so, once rumours started spreading that Jesus had risen, they could simply have produced the body. They didn't, because the body had gone! What is often overlooked by those who believe that the body was stolen is that the grave clothes were left behind. It is difficult to see how this would have happened if the body was stolen, especially as they would have been attached to the corpse by a large quantity of sticky burial spices.

The absence of Jesus from the tomb doesn't, in itself, prove the resurrection, until this is combined with the second fact:

**Jesus' presence with His disciples.** This is of course the major focus of the 40 days. If you piece together the various accounts from the four Gospels, Acts 1 and 1 Corinthians 15, Jesus appeared either to individuals or groups on at least eleven different occasions, numbering well over 500 people. We have concentrated on the major encounters but this is not an exhaustive list. The following resurrection appearances can be identified:

- Resurrection Sunday: Mary Magdalene (John 20:11–18); other women (Matt. 28:9–10); Simon Peter (Luke 24:34; 1 Cor. 15:5); the two on the road to Emmaus (Luke 24:13–35); ten disciples (John 20:19–23; Luke 24:36–43)
- A week later: eleven disciples including Thomas (John 20:24–29)
- Some time later: seven disciples at the Sea of Galilee (John 21); eleven on the mountain (Matt 28:16–20); 500 brothers and sisters (1 Cor. 15:6); James (1 Cor. 15:7)
- Day 40: disciples in Jerusalem (Luke 24:44–49; Acts 1:3–8).
  The overall picture presented to us in the number and variety of

these appearances is that Jesus was very much alive, appearing to them and conversing with His followers as He had before His crucifixion. Moreover, He was clearly the *same* Jesus whom the disciples had known for the previous three and a half years: sufficiently the same for them to recognise both His voice and – after a while – His appearance; living in a body that could be touched, could eat fish and still bore the marks of His crucifixion. Yet He was also somehow different. Not only did the disciples often fail to recognise Him at first, but His body had been transformed in such a way that He was no longer limited by the physical universe and could 'appear' in a room without having to go through the door!

All of this points to a stunning conclusion: the Jesus who had been crucified and lain dead in a tomb for three days, had come back to life. The testimony of the New Testament letters and the book of Revelation, as well as nearly 2,000 years of subsequent Christian history, is that Jesus remains alive today!

## Points to ponder

- With all this evidence in mind, it is worth pausing to reflect and rejoice in the truth that Jesus really is alive.
- If you are not a Christian, today would be a good day to take the first step of inviting the risen Christ to come into your life.
- If you are a Christian but you feel that you've drifted from God, take the time to reaffirm your commitment and decide to live the rest of your life for Him!

## Prayer

*Lord Jesus, I thank You that You have left me with convincing proofs of Your resurrection. I praise You that You rose from the dead and are alive today! Forgive me where I have doubted You, neglected You or gone astray from You. Amen.*

# Day
# 38

## THE FATHER'S PROMISE

## Luke 24:49; Acts 1:4–5

What's the best present you've ever received? My best childhood present was a record player at Christmas in 1972, along with two records: Slade's *Merry Christmas* (mine) and Marie Osmond's *Paper Roses* (my sister's)! In spite of our elation, the fun was only temporary and it certainly didn't change our lives!

On the final day before the ascension, Jesus promised to His disciples a gift that would not only change their lives, but would empower them to go and change the world: 'I am going to send you what my Father promised; but stay in the city until you have been clothed with power from on high' (Luke 24:49). An interesting backdrop to this incident is the Old Testament story of the prophets Elijah and Elisha in 2 Kings 2. Following Elijah's ascension, Elisha picks up his prophet's cloak or mantle which represented the fact that he was to continue to operate in the spirit and power of Elijah (he actually received a double portion of that Spirit!). The parallels are striking. Jesus is like Elijah but greater, in that He had been clothed with God's power (Luke 3:21–22), was mighty in word and deed (Luke 24:19; Acts 10:38), and was about to ascend to heaven. The disciples are like Elisha, waiting and watching Jesus, their 'Elijah', ascend to heaven. They then wait and pray for the promised anointing to come before receiving a mighty outpouring of the Spirit on the Day of Pentecost, ten days later. The language used here is significant: it is as if the Spirit was going to come on the disciples like a cloak ('clothed with power'), and as a result they were going to be able to do and say things that would have been impossible without this 'clothing'.

This promise of the Spirit coming in Luke 24:49, is repeated in Acts 1, but with a different image. (It may well be that, despite differences in language; this is the same event.) Here we read how: 'on one occasion, while he was eating with them he gave them this command: "Do not leave Jerusalem, but wait for the gift my Father promised, which you have heard me speak about. For John baptised with water, but in a few days you will be baptised with the Holy Spirit"' (Acts 1:4–5). This phrase 'baptised with the Holy Spirit' has been highly influential in the history of the church, especially in the last 100 years. The comparison with water baptism is significant. Just as people were immersed by John the Baptist in the River Jordan, so the disciples would be immersed in or with the Holy Spirit by receiving power 'from on high'. If you can imagine standing under the Niagara Falls, it gives some idea of the promise of being drenched with or immersed in the Spirit.

In talking about being 'clothed with power' and 'baptised with the Holy Spirit', Jesus is *not* referring primarily to someone becoming a Christian, but representing an Old Testament emphasis on the *prophetic empowering* of the Spirit, whereby people were able to say and do things as servants of God.

The implications of this are huge. Jesus was promising to His disciples then and now that they can and need to be clothed with power from on high by being baptised with the Holy Spirit. When the Spirit did come on the Day of Pentecost, the 120 followers were all filled with the Holy Spirit (Acts 2:4). Thereafter we see in the book of Acts that this baptism in the Holy Spirit was an event that sometimes occurred simultaneously with conversion (as in Acts 10) and sometimes subsequent to conversion (as in Acts 8 and 19).

This is borne out by the experience of many today. I have seen many filled with the Spirit at Alpha, for example, shortly after or at the point of being converted (or born again). On other occasions, people have a clear time gap from being born again by the Spirit, to being baptised in the Spirit. For some the experience is immediately transformational. For others the event itself is less dramatic but the subsequent changes – a new love for God, a new freedom in prayer, a new hunger for the Bible and a new desire and boldness to tell others about Jesus – are ultimately life-changing. The experiences differ from person to person, but the promise is for all God's children. So, be encouraged by the words of Jesus earlier in the Gospel: 'If you then, though you are evil, know how to give good gifts to your children, how much more will your Father in heaven give the Holy Spirit to those who ask him!' (Luke 11:13).

## Points to ponder

- It may by that you have recently become a Christian, or you may be a long-standing believer, but are conscious that there is something missing. If so, I strongly encourage you to ask your Heavenly Father for His great gift of the Holy Spirit.
- If you have already recieved the power of the Spirit, why not invite the Lord to fill you again today?

## Prayer

*Father, thank You for the wonderful promise of the Holy Spirit. Today I ask You to fill me and re-fill me to overflowing. Let Your Holy Spirit take over every part of my life and all that I do and all that I am, in Jesus' name. Amen.*

# Day

# 39 POWER FOR PURPOSE

## Acts 1:6–8

Here are some famous last words:

'Die, my dear? Why, that's the last thing I'll do!' (Groucho Marx).

'Go on, get out! Last words are for fools who haven't said enough!' (Karl Marx).

'I have not told half of what I saw' (Marco Polo, Venetian traveller and writer).

If you had opportunity to say a few final words to those closest to you before leaving this life on earth, what would they be? Here in Acts we have Jesus' last recorded words before His ascension – unsurprisingly they focus on what He considered to be of utmost importance and were a reminder of what He had already said. In reply to a question from His disciples concerning the restoration of the kingdom to Israel (Acts 1:6) Jesus said: 'It is not for you to know the times or dates the Father has set by his own authority. *But you will receive power when the Holy Spirit comes on you; and you will be my witnesses in Jerusalem, and in all Judea and Samaria, and to the ends of the earth*' (Acts 1:7–8, my emphasis). These are the last words of Jesus on earth. We know this because it says in the very next verse: 'After he said this, he was taken up' (Acts 1:9).

If Jesus considered these final words to be of utmost and final importance it is worth pausing to digest the full implications. First, let's consider the promise: 'you will receive power when the Holy Spirit comes on you'. This is similar in language to what He had already promised concerning being 'clothed with power' and being 'baptised with the Holy Spirit' (see Day 38). Here the same thought is in mind, but with the added emphasis on being *empowered for mission*.

This emphasis on power for purpose is so important. On the one hand many Christians have not availed themselves of this promise of being empowered by the Holy Spirit and are trying to live the Christian life in their own strength. On the other hand, many others who have received this 'Pentecostal' empowering have been intent on enjoying the power and gifts of the Spirit for their own edification, rather than realising that the primary purpose for the Spirit (in the sense that Jesus intended it here) is to empower them to be His witnesses.

The other significant point made in these 'last words' is the fact that the gospel is to be proclaimed to all nations. This has already been declared in the great commission (Matt. 28:19; Mark 16:15). Yet here in Acts 1:8 the worldwide spread of the gospel is emphasised even more clearly (see also Luke 24:47). Starting in Jerusalem, the gospel is then to spread beyond to Judea, Samaria and the ends of the earth. In the context of the Early Church this had both a geographic and demographic fulfillment. Many commentators have noted that Acts 1:8 works as a summary of the rest of the book, with chapters 1–7 focused on Jerusalem, chapter 8 on the expansion into Judea and Samaria and chapter 9 on mission to the Gentiles with the conversion of Saul, leading to his missionary journeys (Acts 13 onwards), and finally to his journey to Rome.

As well as its historical fulfillment in the life of the Early Church, these last words of Jesus have rightly been taken up by many churches and movements as a mandate to reach their local city, town or community, and beyond into their region, nation and the nations. Similarly, this can be applied in the life of individual believers. Each one of us can be Acts 1:8 Christians, living lives empowered by the Holy Spirit and boldly taking the good news in word and deed to those we know (our 'Jerusalem'), as well as to those who are further away from us either relationally or culturally (our 'Judea and Samaria'), and also praying for, giving towards and sometimes going on overseas missions.

What is clear is that these final words of Jesus must be taken very seriously today. Every believer and local church needs to be empowered by the Holy Spirit and fulfill the great commission. If this seems like a repetition of Week 5 of our study, the re-emphasis is deliberate. Before ascending to the Father, Jesus gives His prepared disciples a final reminder: receive the Spirit and go and share the good news to the whole world!

––––

## Points to ponder

- Do you need to ask God for a fresh empowering of Holy Spirit boldness to witness? Why not make it a habit to ask Him for this every day?
- Do you expect the Holy Spirit to work in your life? Could it be that your lack of belief is inhibiting His work through you?
- Make a list of those you know who don't know Jesus, then pray for them, care for them and be ready to share the good news with them.

––––

## Prayer

*Father, I thank You for the power of the Holy Spirit. I ask You to empower me and every member of my local church. Lord, may Your Spirit move in mighty power throughout the Church, both in this nation and across the world! Fill us with boldness that we might take the good news to our community and far beyond. In Jesus' name. Amen!*

# ASCENSION

## Acts 1:9–11; Luke 24:50–51

We finish our 40 days with Jesus as it finished for the disciples: with His ascension to heaven. The ascension is of huge significance in terms of understanding the big story of the Scriptures, but also as it affects our relationship with God the Father, Son and Holy Spirit. The ascension is recorded in both Luke 24 and Acts 1 (and is assumed elsewhere in the New Testament)[24]. The Acts version is the most descriptive, where we read how Jesus was with His disciples when He: 'was taken up before their very eyes, and a cloud hid him before their sight. They were looking intently up into the sky as he was going, when suddenly two men dressed in white stood beside them. "Men of Galilee," they said, "why do you stand here looking into the sky? This same Jesus, who has been taken from you into heaven, will come back in the same way you have seen him go into heaven"' (Acts 1:9–11).

There are two key questions that we must consider: what happened at the ascension and why is it so important?

Let's look briefly at the first question. At first glance the language seems to suggest that Jesus literally ascended, was hidden by a cloud, and was taken 'up' into heaven. However, such geographical language has caused many commentators to question the literalism intended here. The theologian Tom Wright, for example, writes: 'Just as we speak of the sun 'rising', even though we know that the earth is turning in relation to the sun, so ancient Jews were comfortable with the language of heavenly ascent without supposing that their god, and those who shared his habitation, were physically situated a few thousand feet above the surface of the earth.'[25] Wright and others essentially argue that the ascension should be understood theologically rather than geographically, and that earth and heaven are not so much two locations (one physical and the other spiritual), but rather that they are 'two different dimensions of God's good creation'.[26] Whether you agree with this perspective, or adopt a more literal view, one fact is clear: according to the evidence in Luke and Acts 1, the ascension actually took place. Jesus didn't just fade away into some spiritual state. Rather He left this earth as an embodied human being to go to His Father in heaven.

This leads to the second question: why is the ascension so important? There a number of reasons. We will briefly list a few:

- The ascension marked the end of the 40 days and – apart from His appearance to Paul (1 Cor. 15:8) – the end of Christ's physical appearances.
- The ascension signified the crowning of Christ as King. In Peter's Pentecost sermon he boldly declared that the Jesus who was crucified and had been raised from the dead had also ascended and been exalted as 'Lord' (Acts 2:33–36). Jesus is now the ultimate governor or CEO of heaven and earth, ruling and interceding for us at the Father's right hand.
- The ascension ensured that Jesus as both Son of God, and a glorified, resurrected man, is the secure and eternal bridge between us and God, and between heaven and earth (1 Tim. 2:5; Heb. 10:12–14; 19–23).
- The ascension means that Jesus, absent in body, is now ever-present with us by His Spirit (Matt. 28:20 – see Day 35).

The ascension of Jesus is important for one final reason. The fact that Jesus is currently physically absent doesn't mean that He will remain so forever. If we remind ourselves of the words of the angels to the disciples: 'This same Jesus, who has been taken from you into heaven, will come back in the same way you have seen him go into heaven' (Acts 1:11). This means that the great future hope for Christians is not some kind of 'escape' to a spiritualised existence 'in heaven'. Instead our sure hope is that the fully alive and embodied Jesus, who appeared to His disciples during the 40 days, is right now reigning at the Father's right hand and will one day return to bring the full rule of heaven to earth. Those of us who have trusted in Him will live with Him and serve with Him in our resurrected, glorified bodies in heaven on a renewed earth. What a future, what a hope!

## Points to ponder

- How does it change your view of life to know that Jesus is not just alive but is reigning in heaven, and is present with you by His Spirit?
- How does it change your view of the future to know the certainty of Jesus' return to the earth?
- As we conclude our 40 days, take some time to review what you have read and learned. What are the main truths that you have grasped or been reminded about concerning Jesus? How can you live differently for the rest of your life in the light of your answers to these questions?

## Prayer

*Lord, I want to thank You for all that You have revealed to me over the last 40 days. I now ask for Your Spirit to help me remember and grow in an ever-deepening relationship with You. My life is Yours and always will be. Empower me now to go and make a difference to the world around me, in Jesus' name, Amen!*

# NOTES

[1] Some of the earliest manuscripts do not include 16:9–20.

[2] The evidence that Jesus rose from the dead is indeed hugely compelling, and has received extensive scholarly support, both ancient and modern. One of the most recent studies is the very comprehensive work by N.T. Wright, *The Resurrection of the Son of God* (SPCK, 2003).

[3] Dr. Gary Habermas, 'The Resurrection Evidence that changed a Generation of Scholars' lecture, 13 March 2008 in Westminster Chapel, London (cf. Richard Bauckham, *Jesus and the Eyewitnesses* (William B Eerdmans, 2008)).

[4] The appearance of Jesus to the apostle Paul (1 Cor. 15:8) seems to have been an isolated and special incident outside of the 40 Days and the last of Jesus' physical appearances to His disciples, prior to His second coming.

[5] Matthew 28:1; Mark 16:1; Luke 24:1. This is confirmed indirectly in John 20:2, where Mary refers to others with her.

[6] It is noteworthy that when Paul describes to the Corinthians the witnesses to the resurrection (1 Cor. 15) he omits the women. Presumably, he knew that their testimony would not carry weight.

[7] This can only mean that the other disciple believed that Jesus was risen. He becomes the antithesis to Thomas later in the chapter (see Days 20–21).

[8] This is often seen as an allusion to the two cherubim on the Ark of the Covenant.

[9] J. Packer, *Knowing God* (Hodder and Stoughton, 1993) p232.

[10] For this vital concept of the exchange of the cross see a few of many examples (Rom. 4:24 ; 5:9; 1 Pet. 2:24; 2 Cor. 5:21; 2 Cor. 8:9)

[11] Jesus does condemn them as foolish (not in the sense of being stupid, but as being obtuse or slow to understand) but only because they have failed to successfully understand the Old Testament verses, eg 2 Samuel 7:12–16; Isaiah 7:14; 9:6; 52:13–53:12; Jeremiah 23:5–6; Daniel 7:13–14; Daniel 9:24–27.

[12] Nicky Gumbel, *Questions of Life* (Kingsway, 1993) p84.

[13] Duncan Bannatyne, *Anyone Can Do It* (Orion, 2006) p231ff.

[14] The parallel with Eden is heightened if, as is not unreasonably supposed, they were husband and wife.

[15] Peace is also linked in John's Gospel with the Holy Spirit (see John 14:26–27).

[16] J. Blank, *Krisis* (Freiburg: Lambertus, 1964) p178, op. cit., B. Milne, *The Message of John* (IVP, 1993) p298.

[17] There is an important point here about not being too super spiritual; even the most saintly people must eat.

[18] We have references (Luke 24:34; 1 Cor. 15:5) that Jesus appeared to Peter on Easter Sunday but no record of what took place.

[19] Actually for many Christians the real problem is not the way that they are called to die (that tends to be a fairly brief process) but the way that they are called to live (that is a very drawn out business).

[20] Rick Warren, *The Purpose Driven Life* (Zondervan, 2002) p17

[21] The existence of such an embarrassing phrase is a strong indicator of the authenticity of this event. If, as some people claim, the Gospels are late inventions of the church, who on earth would include such language?

[22] D.A. Carson *Expositor's Bible Commentary* v8 ed. Frank Gaebelein (Zondervan, 1984) pp594.

[23] This is a 'Son of Man' claim, alluding to Daniel 7:13–14.

[24] See for example: Romans 8:34; Ephesians 1:20–23; 2:6; 4:8–11; Philippians 2:6–11; 1 Timothy 3:16; Hebrews 1:3.

[25] N.T. Wright, *The Resurrection of the Son of God* (Fortress Press, 2003) p655.

[26] Tom Wright, *Surprised by Hope* (SPCK, 2007) p122.

## 40 DAYS WITH JESUS COMES WITH FREE SERMON OUTLINES, SMALL GROUP STUDIES AND VIDEO TEACHING.

### Visit www.40days.info to find out more.

## 01 For you

Be strengthened in your walk with God as you read this 40-day devotional. Explore the life-changing encounters that biblical characters had with the risen Jesus.

## 02 For your small group

Free online video teaching and study guides to help your small group learn and share together as you work through the book.

## 03 For your church

Free online sermon outlines for church leaders – exploring each of the six encounters highlighted in the devotional book and small group resources.

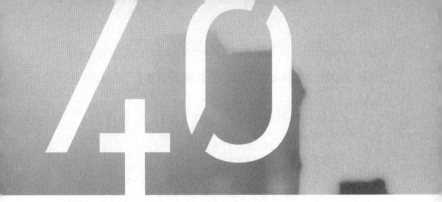

# What happens next?

## 01 Sign up

Sign up at **www.40days.info** and we will keep you up to date with all the latest news and developments. We'll also send you a free welcome pack for your church.

## 02 Invite

Once you have decided to take part, invite your church to join in. This is an exciting journey and a great opportunity to engage with friends and guests.

## 03 Order

The 40-day devotional is designed to underpin the whole series. To order bulk copies for your church or small group visit **www.cwr.org.uk/40days**

# Is it possible to be hugely blessed by God and still make a mess of your life?

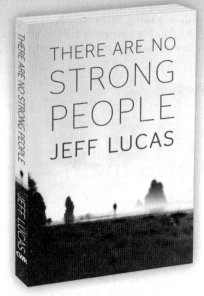

In this provocative, breathtakingly honest book on the Bible's infamous rascal, Samson, Jeff Lucas explores some vital principles for living life well.

- What is it we all really crave?
- Do good people do bad things?
- What do we do when we're disappointed?
- Are there clear steps towards success – and disaster?

This is a book that asks its readers to think, re-evaluate and dig deeper. Anyone who chooses to take up this challenge won't be disappointed.

*There Are No Strong People*
by Jeff Lucas
ISBN: 978-1-85345-624-4

**Accompanying four session DVD available.**

# Know God better and be strengthened spiritually

Our compact, daily Bible reading notes for adults are published bimonthly and offer a focus for every need. They are available as individual issues or annual subscriptions, in print, in ebook format or by email.

## Every Day with Jesus

With around half a million readers, this insightful devotional by Selwyn Hughes is one of the most popular daily Bible reading tools in the world. A large-print edition is also available. 72-page booklets, 120x170mm

## Inspiring Women Every Day

Written by women for women to inspire, encourage and strengthen. 64-page booklets, 120x170mm

## Life Every Day

Apply the Bible to life each day with these challenging life-application notes written by international speaker and well-known author Jeff Lucas. 64-page booklets, 120x170mm

## Cover to Cover Every Day

Study one Old Testament and one New Testament book in depth with each issue, and a psalm every weekend. Two well-known Bible scholars each contribute a month's series of daily Bible studies. Covers every book of the Bible in five years. 64-page booklets, 120x170mm

For current price and to order visit **www.cwr.org.uk/subscriptions**

Also available online or from Christian bookshops

Courses and seminars

Publishing and media

Conference facilities

# Transforming lives

CWR's vision is to enable people to experience personal transformation through applying God's Word to their lives and relationships.

Our Bible-based training and resources help people around the world to:
• Grow in their walk with God
• Understand and apply Scripture to their lives
• Resource themselves and their church
• Develop pastoral care and counselling skills
• Train for leadership
• Strengthen relationships, marriage and family life and much more.

 **CWR** Applying God's Word
*to everyday life and relationships*

CWR, Waverley Abbey House,
Waverley Lane, Farnham,
Surrey GU9 8EP, UK

Telephone: +44 (0)1252 784700
Email: info@cwr.org.uk
Website: www.cwr.org.uk

Registered Charity No 294387
Company Registration No 1990308

Our insightful writers provide daily Bible-reading notes and other resources for all ages, and our experienced course designers and presenters have gained an international reputation for excellence and effectiveness.

CWR's Training and Conference Centres in Surrey and East Sussex, England, provide excellent facilities in idyllic settings – ideal for both learning and spiritual refreshment.